
A guide to the West Midland Way

A guide to

the West Midland Way

Ron Leek and Eric Jones

Constable London

First published in Great Britain 1979
by Constable and Company Ltd
10 Orange Street London WC2H 7EG

ISBN 0 09 462790 8

Set in Monophoto Times New Roman 9pt
Filmset and printed in Great Britain by
BAS Printers Limited, Over Wallop, Hampshire

	Foreword	9
	Acknowledgements	10
	Introduction	11
	How to use the guide	13
	Equipment	15
	Obstruction of rights of way	19
1	Meriden – Berkswell – Kenilworth	23
2	Kenilworth – Honiley – Wroxall – Rowington – Lowsonford – Preston Bagot – Henley in Arden	39
3	Henley in Arden – Ullenhall – Alvechurch	57
4	Alvechurch – Cofton Hackett – Lickey Hills – Clent Hills – Adams Hill	71
5	Adams Hill – Holy Cross – Broome – Churchill – Caunsall – Kinver Edge	85
6	Kinver – The Sheepwalks – Birdsgreen – Hampton Loade – Chelmarsh – Bridgnorth	97
7	Bridgnorth – Worfield – Ackleton – Badger – Beckbury – Ryton – Tong	115
8	Tong – Boscobel – Bishops Wood – Lapley – Longnor – Bradley – Coppenhall – Dunston – Acton Trussell – Bednall – Brocton	129
9	Cannock Chase including Shugborough and Great Haywood	147
10	Gentleshaw – Creswell Green – Farewell – Elmhurst – Streethay – Whittington	161
11	Whittington – Hints – Drayton Bassett – Middleton – Bodymoor Heath – Kingsbury	173
12	Kingsbury – Hurley – Nether Whitacre – Botts Green – Church End – Maxstoke – Meriden	189
	Index	208

Illustrations

Meriden Cross, at the centre of England	25
Footpath sign, near Berkswell	27
St John the Baptist, Berkswell	29
Kenilworth Castle	34
Church Green, Kenilworth	36
St Nicholas, Kenilworth	36
Backward glance to Kenilworth Castle	41
St John the Baptist, Honiley	43
Lock and bridge, Stratford on Avon Canal	47
Old Barn, near Preston Bagot	49
South doorway, St Nicholas, Beaudesert	52
Henley-in-Arden, St John the Baptist and Guildhall	53
Market Cross, Henley-in-Arden	54
Ullenhall Village	60
St Mary's, Ullenhall	61
St Laurence, Alvechurch	67
The Old House, Alvechurch	68
Worcester and Birmingham Canal, near Bittell	73
Standing Stones, Clent Hill	79
Near summit of Clent Hill	80
North West from Clent Hill	81
Folly at Adams Hill	82
St Peter's, Broome	87
Footpath to Churchill	88
Slot Stile, near Churchill	89
River Stour, Caunsall	91
Rock dwelling, Holy Austin Rock, Kinver	93
Into Lakehouse Dingle	102
Waterfall, Lakehouse Dingle	103
Chain ferry across River Severn	105
Severn Valley Railway	106
The leaning keep, Bridgnorth Castle	111
Northgate, Bridgnorth	113
River Worfe and old mill wheel	117
Entrance to Worfield	119

Worfield village 120
St Giles, Badger 122
St Bartholomew's, Tong 126
Hubbal Grange 131
White Ladies Priory 131
The Royal Oak, Boscobel 132
Notice on the Royal Oak 133
Black Ladies 134
The Webb Stone, Bradley 138
In Bradley Village 140
Sherbrook Valley 149
Triumphal Arch, Shugborough 151
Tower of the Winds, Shugborough 153
Shugborough Hall 153
Essex Bridge 154
Trent and Mersey Canal, near Colwich 155
Inn sign, Gentleshaw 159
Farewell Hall 163
View towards Rugeley from near Elmhurst 165
Near Streethay 168
St Bartholomew's, Hints 177
Roundhill Wood 178
Langley Brook, footbridge with stiles 182
Footway towards Kingsbury 184
Kingsbury Hall 185
Church End, Shustoke 196
Maxstoke Priory 199
Walsh Hall 204
Return to Meriden Cross 206

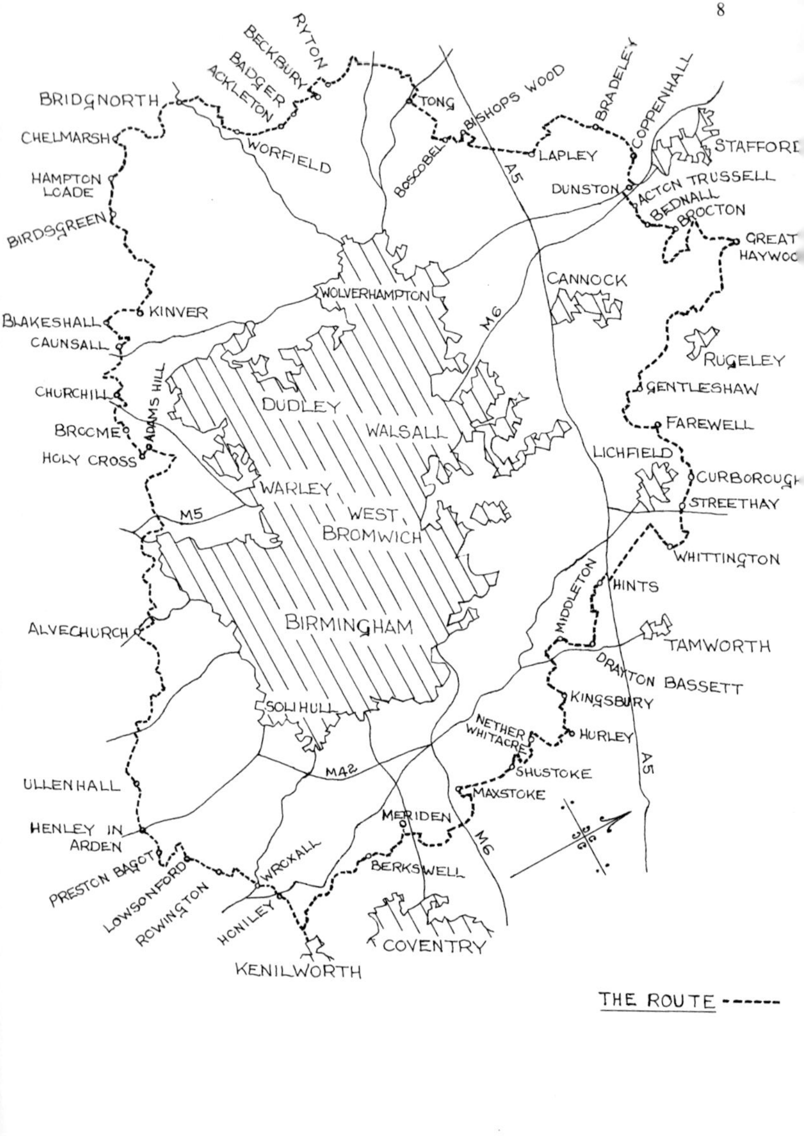
BRIDGNORTH
ACKLETON
BADGER
BECKBURY
RYTON
TONG
BISHOPS WOOD
BOSCOBEL
BRADELEY
COPPENHALL
LAPLEY
STAFFORD
DUNSTON
ACTON TRUSSELL
BEDNALL
BROCTON
GREAT HAYWOOD
WORFIELD
A5
CHELMARSH
HAMPTON LOADE
BIRDSGREEN
KINVER
BLAKESHALL
CAUNSALL
CHURCHILL
BROOME
HOLY CROSS
ADAMS HILL
WOLVERHAMPTON
CANNOCK
M6
RUGELEY
GENTLESHAW
FAREWELL
DUDLEY
WALSALL
LICHFIELD
CURBOROUGH
STREETHAY
WARLEY
WEST BROMWICH
M5
WHITTINGTON
HINTS
MIDDLETON
BIRMINGHAM
ALVECHURCH
TAMWORTH
DRAYTON BASSETT
KINGSBURY
SOLIHULL
NETHER WHITACRE
HURLEY
A5
M42
SHUSTOKE
MAXSTOKE
ULLENHALL
MERIDEN
HENLEY IN ARDEN
M6
WROXALL
BERKSWELL
PRESTON BAGOT
LOWSONFORD
ROWINGTON
HONILEY
COVENTRY
KENILWORTH

THE ROUTE ------

Foreword

by Vivian Bird

For twenty-five years, as a feature-writer who wrote on my feet, I spent much time devising and undertaking unusual walks. There were gimmicky walks—Purgatory, an Oxfordshire farm, to Paradise, a Gloucestershire hamlet, 45 miles/72·4 km across the Cotswolds; celebration walks—Waterloo Road in south Birmingham, 22 miles/35·4 km to St Helena, Polesworth, on the 150th anniversary of the Battle of Waterloo in 1965; personal walks—50 miles/80·4 km in 17 hours 15 minutes on my fiftieth birthday; and stamina testing walks—my 'Six Shropshire Summits', 35 miles/56·3 km across the six Shropshire hills exceeding 1,500 feet/457·2 m, now nationally famous, which for completing in under 20 hours some 1,800 walkers have received a certificate.

Then there were the longer serial walks, 250 miles/402·3 km or so round the boundaries of Warwickshire, Worcestershire, and Staffordshire, done at 20 miles/32·3 km a day. These gave a splendid insight into the character of each county.

The West Midland Way is not dissimilar as a walking concept of encircling an area. It does differ, however, in offering a complete contrast to the territory circumambulated. The new West Midlands Metropolitan County, generally execrated by traditionalists, is a massive conurbation of Birmingham, Wolverhampton, the Black Country, and Coventry, but this walk around it traverses delightful countryside, so charmingly described in the authors' Introduction, that one wishes for more such writing within the book.

That, however, is not the authors' intent; they are there as guides not interpreters. Having determined where to go from their impeccable directions, the walker can find sufficient books descriptive of any section of the walk.

Eric Jones and Ron Leek are to be commended for their ingenuity in conceiving the West Midland Way; for their perseverance in following it; and for their patient and exact committal of the route to the printed page.

The authors would like to thank the following persons and organizations for willing help given before, or whilst, preparing this book.

The staffs of the Planning/Countryside Departments of: Shropshire County Council, Staffordshire County Council, Warwickshire County Council, West Midlands County Council, Worcestershire County Council, the staff of Boscobel House, Shropshire, the staff of the Midland Roads Construction Unit.

Vivian Bird, Midlands author, journalist and broadcaster, for the Foreword, and his enthusiastic advice and guidance.

Fellow traveller, young Charles Leek for his companionship and assistance.

The 1:100000 maps appear at the beginning of each section and are reproduced with the permission of Messrs. Bartholomew.

The West Midland Way is the description of a circular walk, which in winding its way through the counties of Shropshire, Staffordshire, Warwickshire, West Midlands, and Worcestershire, completely encircles the larger western conurbation of the West Midlands Metropolitan County, passing between this and the smaller eastern section.

Immediately beyond the boundaries of this vast residential and industrial complex, encompassing the major cities and boroughs of Birmingham, Wolverhampton, Walsall, Warley, West Bromwich, Dudley, and Solihull, some of the most delightful countryside in England is to be found.

Varying between hills, heathland, rolling pastureland, and quiet riverside meadows, the country through which the walk passes presents an ever-changing kaleidoscope of form, colour, texture, and atmosphere. You are led through charming towns and villages, picturesque with their black and white half-timbered work, and thatched-roof cottages; by byways and field paths, beside fields of waving corn; through sun-dappled woodland, heady with the scent of pine; along the bottom of steep-sided dingles, carpeted with a profusion of brilliant wild flowers; into quiet churchyards, and ancient churches; past farms and yards piled high with new-mown hay; along lazy canals, with only a moorhen to create the slightest ripple; up to windswept heights on rugged hills, where seemingly endless vistas sweep away to the horizon: all these, and more, await your pleasure.

From the heights of the Lickeys, the Clents, Kinver Edge, and Cannock Chase, you can gaze across the whole beautiful scene. In the old towns of Bridgnorth and Kenilworth, you can look back into time, to the history of our forefathers; at Boscobel, who has not heard of the oak tree in which King Charles II hid while escaping from the Battle of Worcester? Industrial landscapes take on a mellow and pleasing aspect when viewed from the distant slopes of Gentleshaw Hill, and the Severn, that most noble of rivers known to the Romans as

Sabrina, you cross by an old chain ferry, to walk where enthusiasts eagerly journey in preserved steam trains on the restored Severn Valley Railway . . . These then are just a few of the delights that you see and visit while following the described route. Villages, churches, houses, scenery, points of interest, and historical facts along the way are briefly described in the text of the walk. Similarly, inns and cafés on or near the route receive mentions, both as references, and more importantly, as places of refreshment.

The walk, described in a clockwise direction, follows definitive Public Rights of Way throughout, and except for continuity, utilizes roads and lanes as little as possible. It is 162 miles/261 km in length, and runs at the most 12 miles/19 km, and at the least immediately outside, the boundary of the built-up area. At all points it is easily accessible by both public and private transport.

For any circular walk it is difficult to define a start and finish, but in this instance, as the walk passes between the two great conurbations of Birmingham and Coventry, there is an obvious starting-point for this written description. This is of course Meriden, the traditional centre of England, which as such is already renowned.

The old cross then, marking the centre of England and standing proudly on the green in the village of Meriden, is the starting point for our walk, and when after many enchanting miles, we finally return, it also marks the finish.

All instructions regarding right or left are given as seen in the direction of the walk. The words 'towards', 'bear', 'bearing', etc, when related to a change of direction, indicate a turn which is less than a full 90-degree right-angled turn, and unless further qualified by words such as 'slightly', can be taken as approximately 45 degrees.

Unless otherwise stated, when walking along the edge of a field and approaching a corner, all gates, stiles, etc, mentioned in the text, are directly in front, on the edge of the field towards which one is walking.

In several instances very busy main railway-lines are crossed. *Extreme* caution is necessary at these places, because with modern track, or electrification, trains approach fairly noiselessly at very high speeds.

The following terms are generally used throughout this book, and should be interpreted as indicated:

Gateway – the opening in a fence, hedge, or wall, where a gate, and/or gateposts may or may not be present.
Intruding Field Corner – the corner of a fence, hedge, or wall, where this projects into the area of the field.
Double Hedges or Gates – two hedges or gates in close succession across the line of our path.
Cross Track – a track running across the line of our path.
Temporary Fence – a fairly recently erected fence, which may or may not be of a permanent nature, which does not appear on the Definitive Footpath Maps held by the County Councils.

It must be borne in mind at all times, that this detailed description of the route could be subject to change due to many factors, such as the grubbing out of hedges, enlarging of fields, removal of gates, erection of new fences, building of properties, creation of housing estates, road improvements, etc. Also, as the West Midland Way is not an officially recognized route, there could be the possibility of minor changes to some sections of the path. The authors, therefore, wish to point out that in following this guide, the walker must make due allowance when meeting any such alterations, and they hope that the enjoyment of the walk is in no way impaired thereby.

If the prospective walker is wise, he or she will give due consideration to the question of equipment. Everyone knows how our weather smiles only to deceive. We start out on a day bright with sunshine, only to suffer the deluge later.

Boots

These are of course the most important item, and you will have no problems if correctly shod with a stout pair of walking boots. These are preferable to heavy shoes which do not give the ankle the support that is so often needed over uneven ground.

Once your boots are oiled and broken in, they will become your stout companions for many miles, and no other footwear is more comfortable.

It is advisable to have half a size larger than your normal shoe size. This will enable you to wear two pairs of woollen socks, which will virtually eliminate any chafing around the back of the heels. Good walking boots are expensive these days, but you will be more than repaid in the long term by their comfort and service.

Clothing

Perhaps more a question of personal taste, but there is no doubt that a special walking zip-jacket, or anorak with hood and plenty of pockets for maps etc, have their advantages, in that they are comfortable to wear, and both windproof and reasonably showerproof. Slacks worn with the bottoms tucked into the socks are excellent, although some may prefer a pair of walking breeches similar to those worn by climbers. These also are good, and perhaps even preferable, because they allow more freedom around the feet.

Pullovers

This again is a matter of preference, but we feel it advisable that you should at least carry a lightweight woollen long-sleeved pullover in your rucksack in case it turns very cold.

Waterproofs
There are some excellent ultra-lightweight, nylon, hooded, zip-waterproofs now available, that can be worn over your anorak in the event of prolonged walking in the rain. These will fold up small enough to fit into a pocket of either jacket or rucksack. If you prefer greater coverage, then a knee-length cagoule made of the same lightweight material would be suitable.

Rucksack
This is of course a necessary item of your kit, and can be obtained in a variety of shapes, sizes, and weights.

For day walking, a small light type will give satisfactory service. An ideal choice would be a light alloy tubular frame, on to which can be attached a small light nylon rucksack. The frame keeps the sack off the back, and so allows ample ventilation.

Maps
Although a map is not absolutely necessary when you follow our steps with this book, it can be worthwhile to carry the Ordnance Survey 1:50,000 First Series map, choosing of course the section which adequately covers the area through which you are walking.

You may wish to curtail a section of our route for some reason, and then the Ordnance Survey map would be invaluable to get you back to civilization.

The route of the 'West Midland Way' is covered by the following numbered Ordnance Survey maps:

1:50,000 series
127, 128, 138, 139, 140, 150, 151.

1:25,000 Series
SJ70, SJ80, SJ81, SJ91, SJ92,
SK01, SK02, SK10, SK11,
SO78, SO79, SO87, SO88, SO97, SO98,
SP06, SP07, SP16, SP19, SP26, SP27, SP28, SP29.

Compass

This is always worth including in your walking equipment, and although you may seldom need it when walking with this book, perhaps there will be an occasion when fog or heavy mist comes down and you cannot see your objective. You can then take a bearing from the Ordnance Survey map—the 1:25,000 First or Second Series are especially good for this—and walk along the indicated bearing. This will ensure that you maintain the correct direction and right of way. In any case, there is something very satisfying in walking a bearing when landmarks are obscured, and finding that you come out exactly where planned.

Symbols used on sketch maps

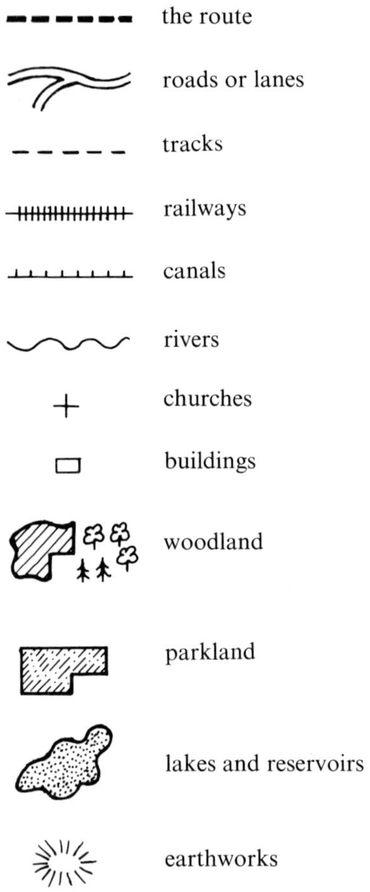

The Rights of Way followed in this book may at times be obstructed in places. A bone fide traveller has a legal right to remove the obstruction if necessary in order to get by, provided that *only* as much as is necessary to get by is removed.

Common forms of obstruction are: barbed wire across the Right of Way; misleading notices, e.g. *Private*; locked gates across the Right of Way; overgrowth, undergrowth, and hedges blocking the Right of Way; crops planted across the Right of Way—unless a temporary diversion notice is prominently posted, the right action is to walk through the crop in single file along the Right of Way, causing no unnecessary damage.

See also: *A practical guide to the Law of Footpaths and Bridleways*, by Ian Campbell LLB, published by the Commons, Open Spaces and Footpaths Preservation Society; and *Right of Way*, published by the Ramblers' Association.

Guard against all risk of fire
Fasten all gates
Keep dogs under proper control
Keep to the paths across farm land
Avoid damaging fences, hedges and walls
Leave no litter
Safeguard water supplies
Protect wild life, wild plants, and trees
Go carefully on country roads
Respect the life of the countryside

Meriden
Forest Hall
Cross
B 4102
A 45
Eaves Green
Hawkes End
Pickford
Alton Ho.
Pickford Green
Pickford Brook
Cornets End
Four Oaks
131m
Upper Eastern Green
Flint's Green
Hockley
Bradnocks Marsh
The Moat
Benton Green
Berkswell
Wootton Green
Blythe Ho.
Ram Hall
A 4023
Tile Hill
BERKSWELL STA
Carol Green
Balsall Common
Beechwood
Westwood Heath
Balsall
Sedgemere
Fen End
Holly Grange
128m
A 452
Meer End
Rudfyn Manor
Finham Brook
The Spri
A 4177
Kenilworth
Kenilworth Cas
Grounds
Ford
Haseley Knob
Bockendon Grange

1 Meriden – Berkswell – Kenilworth

Distance: 8¼ miles/13·25 km

Starting from Meriden's medieval cross which traditionally marks the centre of England, walk along the old village green, and passing the Cyclists' Memorial continue down the main road through the village for approximately a ¼-mile/400 m, to the Bulls Head Inn. Turning right opposite here, walk for a few yards along the tarmac driveway leading into the grounds of Meriden Hall, and just before the gateway turn right along the fenced gravel footpath. At the end of this turn left through the kissing-gate, and walk across the field, veering slightly away from a parallel to the left-hand edge. Cross the stile in front, and walk straight across the next field, noting the eighteenth-century Meriden Hall through the trees to the left. Pass to the right of the lone tree and cross the stile in front, some yards to the right of the corner. Walk straight ahead up the field, heading for the large chestnut tree which can be seen above the skyline; initially passing a few yards to the right of a walled intruding corner.

From the vantage point at the top of the field, a magnificent panoramic view is seen across to the right, with the Birmingham conurbation around which you are walking, prominent centrally. The Lickey and Clent Hills are seen to its left, and Cannock Chase is visible away to the right.

Bearing left, cross the stile a few yards before the chestnut tree at the field corner, and walk straight across the following field, passing a few yards to the right of the solitary pine. The distant tower of Meriden church is seen just to the left of this. Continue ahead from here, and cross the stile in the hedge in front.

Crossing the lane and the piece of fence opposite into the field, walk alongside the very short piece of hedge on the left, and then bearing left, continue diagonally across to the opposite corner. Cross the fence on the left of this, and turning right, walk along the hedged path. Cross the stile at its end into the corner of the field. Turning towards the left,

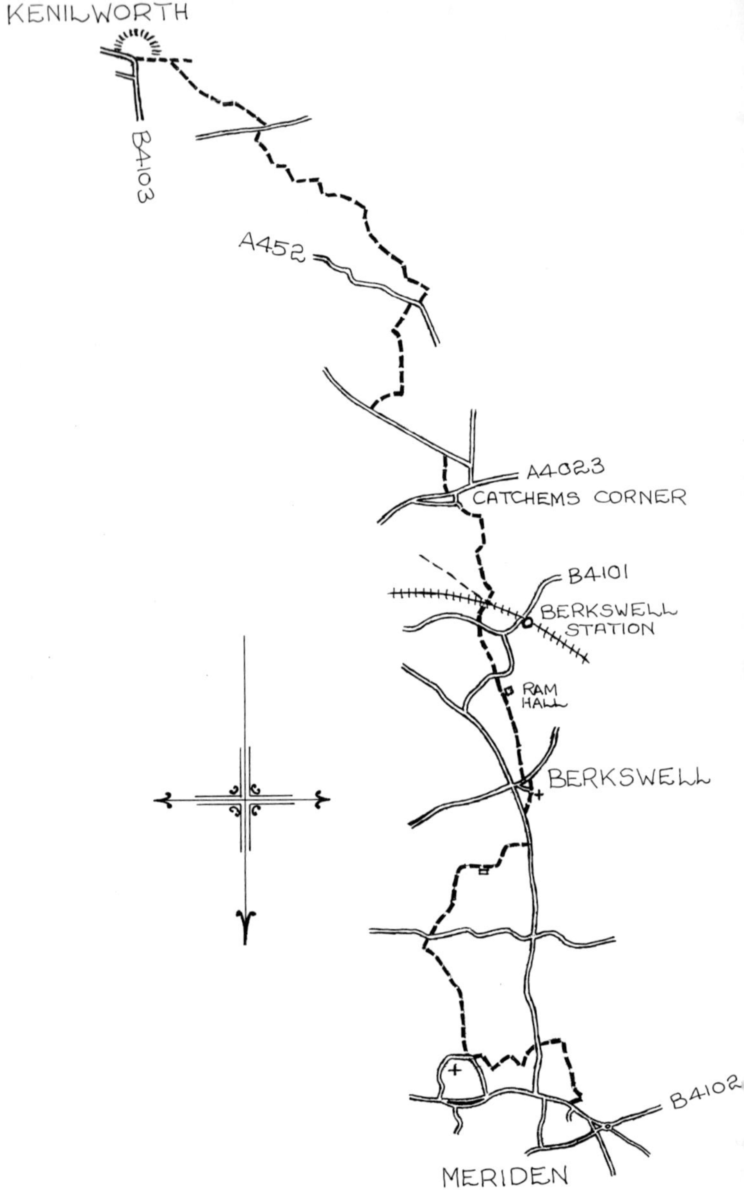
KENILWORTH
B4103
A452
A4023
CATCHEMS CORNER
B4101
BERKSWELL STATION
RAM HALL
BERKSWELL
B4102
MERIDEN

Meriden Cross, at the centre of England

walk diagonally across this, heading towards the gateway which can be seen at the bottom of the field beyond, just before two dormer bungalows in the line of houses below. Approximately halfway across the first field, turn right and walk diagonally back up the field, heading for the small piece of fence in what is now the left-hand hedge, approximately 40 yards/37 m down from the top corner. Cross this, and continue diagonally across the next field to the piece of fence in the hedge just to the right of the top left-hand corner. Crossing this, turn left and walk along the edge of the next field, shortly crossing a temporary fence running up it. Arriving in the corner alongside the electricity pole, bear right and continue up the next edge of the field. After about 150 yards/137 m and at a slight corner, cross the fence on the left, and walk along the hedged track. At the end of this, arrive at a bend in the lane running up from Meriden village.

By continuing straight ahead up this lane, St Laurence's church can be visited at the top of the hill. This has a Norman chancel, and the rest is mainly fourteenth and fifteenth century. Just outside the churchyard gate is an old stepped horse-mounting block.

Immediately at the aforementioned bend in the lane, turn across the fence on the right into the field. Bearing slightly to the left, walk diagonally across the field, heading just to the right of the double electricity pole seen in front. Bear right at the fence and follow the left-hand edge of this very large field. A few yards before reaching the end of this, bear right and walk diagonally across the corner to the stile in front, leading into the right-hand of the two following fields. Cross the ditch and then this stile, and walk along the left-hand edge of the field. Go through the gateway, and turning towards the left, walk diagonally across the end of the next field, to the gateway on the right of the opposite corner. Go through this, and walk up the left-hand edge of the following field. Where the edge of this bears slightly away to the left, continue ahead across the corner to the gateway in front. Pass through this, and, initially walking alongside the hedge on the right, continue straight up the field, heading just to the left of the electricity pole which can be seen above the skyline. The pole itself is some way to the left of the just-visible farmhouse chimneys. Cross the fence in front at the top of the field, and continue ahead across the next, heading for the gateway at the corner just to the left of the barn at Wakelins Farm. Go through this, and walk along the short hedged track.

Cross the lane at the end of the track, and going through the gateway opposite, walk along the left-hand edge of the field. At the corner of this, pass a pond on the left and cross the small piece of fence in the hedge. Walk along the right-hand edge of the following field, and passing through the gateway, continue along the right-hand edge of the next field. Pass a pond on the right in the corner, and cross the small piece of fence in front, into the corner of the next field. Turning towards the left, walk ahead into the field, passing to the left of the pond. Immediately after this, bear slightly towards the right and walk across to the far right-hand corner; this heading is just to the left of the cottage which is seen beyond. Turn through the gateway on the right, and walk along the fenced and hedged track known as Blind Lane, that passes in front of the cottage. Continue along this track, passing the old half-timbered Blind Hall Farm, to the gateway at its end. Go through this, and turn left along the road towards Berkswell village.

Footpath sign, near Berkswell

Approximately 50 yards/46 m before reaching the first houses on the left, turn through the kissing-gate on the right, and walk along the fenced path through the narrow belt of woodland. After some yards this bears left, and runs along the edge of the woodland towards Berkswell church, which is seen directly in front. Berkswell Hall is the large house in the parkland across to the right. Go through the gateway at the end of the path, and walk along the left-hand edge of the churchyard. Note the unusual stone war memorial in the form of a small Gothic pavilion.

The church of St John the Baptist is recognized as the most interesting Norman village church in Warwickshire. It has an impressive vaulted crypt under the fine Norman chancel, with a unique octagonal extension. The north nave arcade is also of this same period. The two-storied timber south porch with its open tracery sides is sixteenth century, and the tower, with its sundial larger than the clock, is late-fifteenth century.

A few yards into the village along Church Lane are the old stocks on the village green—but why *five* holes? A little way further, at the crossroads, is the Bear Inn.

Leaving the churchyard by the iron kissing-gate in the corner, at the end of the path we were following, cross straight over the end of Church Lane and walk along the path opposite, passing between the two wooden posts. Berks Well is the large rectangular stone basin immediately on the right at the start of this path. Passing between a line of four posts, the path continues as a short track to Lavender Hall Lane. Turn left along this for a few yards, and then turn right along the tarmac footpath leading through the arch immediately at the left-hand end of the block of four bungalows. The village green is just a few yards to the left at this point.

Walk along the short hedged path and, crossing the fence at the end, walk along the right-hand end of the field. Go through the gateway, and continue along the right-hand edge of the following field. Pass through the gateway and follow the right-hand edge of the next field, to a point approximately 17 yards/15·5 m before its end and just after the end of the

St John the Baptist, Berkswell

field on the right. Turn right across the fence here, into the corner of the next field, and still continuing in the previous direction, walk along the left-hand edge of this. Turn right in the corner at the bottom of the field, and walk alongside the hedge on the left for approximately 40 yards/37 m, and then turning left, cross the fence into the corner of the right-hand of the two fields. Walk up the left-hand edge of this, and go through the gateway. Continue straight ahead along the next field, keeping parallel to its right-hand edge. Just over halfway up the field, go through the gateway in front alongside the farm buildings. Continue ahead across the end of the farmyard, with the early seventeenth-century Ram Hall to the right; and passing through the gateway in front, walk along the hedged and fenced track.

At the end of the track cross the lane, and go through the gateway opposite, just to the left of the pond. Walk straight ahead down the field in front, heading for the stile which can be seen at a kink in the bottom edge, just to the left of the small gnarled oak. Just before reaching the stile, walk alongside the short piece of hedge on the right. Cross the stiles and the tiny stream between them, and continue straight across the next field to the intruding corner in front, coming from the left. Pass to the right of this, and walk alongside the hedge and fence on the left to the corner. Cross the fence, and continue along the left-hand edge of the next field. At the end of this, cross the fence into the corner of the next field, and turning slightly towards the right, walk diagonally across this field to the small piece of fence approximately halfway along the edge in front.

Cross the fence, and continuing straight over the B4101 road, walk along the hedged path directly opposite. (There are the remains of a stile at this point.) The path almost immediately turns left, and then bears round towards the right, passing the gardens of a house. Continue along this path which is now both hedged and fenced, and passing through the small area of bushes at its end, cross the fence in front, and walk diagonally to the right across the main Birmingham–London railway-line. Continue ahead along the short left-hand end of the triangular area of land lying between the junction of the line we have just crossed, and the track of the old line, which ran to Kenilworth, away to the left. Cross this track, and the siding which still runs along it for a short distance, and dropping down the bank, cross the fence and footbridge over the small stream.

Turning towards the left, walk diagonally across the field to the opposite corner. Go through the gateway on the left of this, and walk along the right-hand edge of the next field. Approximately 50 yards/46 m before reaching the corner, turn through the gateway on the right. Immediately turn left and walk along the left-hand edge of the field, initially cutting across a slight corner to the intruding corner just in front.

Cross the fence and walk along the left-hand edge of the next field. Pass to the left of a pond at the end of this, and cross the fence. Continue along the left-hand edge of the next one, crossing the remains of an old stile at its end. Turning towards the right, walk diagonally across the following field to the opposite corner. Cross the fence on the right of this, and turning left in the corner of the next field, walk along its left-hand edge. Cross the fence, and walk along the left-hand end of the narrow field. Cross the plank bridge over the small muddy stream just to the right of the corner in front, and continue straight across the next field to the opposite corner. Avoiding the stile in front at this corner, turn across the fence on the left, and walk along the right-hand edge of the following field. After approximately 70 yards/64 m, turn across the fence on the right, and walk along the hedged path. At the end of this, bear left between the cottages, and proceed along the short roadway to the bend in Waste Lane. Bear right along this, and at the end turn left along the main A4023 road.

Almost immediately, turn right through the gateway on the left of Mulberry Cottage which is opposite, and walk along the right-hand end of the field. Go through the gateway immediately alongside the cottage, and continue along the right-hand edge of the next field. After approximately 60 yards/55 m, where the hedge and fence turn away to the right, continue straight ahead across the narrow neck in the field to the gateway in front, just to the left of the intruding corner. Go through this gateway, and walk along the right-hand edge of the field. Pass to the right of the farm building at the end of the field, and then turn left between it and the small wooden building. Immediately bear right, and walk diagonally across the small area of ground to the roadway running through the farm complex. Bear right along this roadway, and walk between the buildings of Camp Farm, passing through a gateway to the left of the farmhouse.

At the end of this roadway, turn left and walk along Hob Lane for approximately a ½-mile/800 m. Some yards after passing under the electricity power lines, turn right through the gateway immediately after a cottage on the right, and opposite the Burton Green village nameplate. Walk along the hedged and fenced tarmac roadway. Just before reaching the modern house at the end of this, go through the gateway directly in front at the kink in the right-hand hedge. Continue along the left-hand edge of the field. After a short distance, turn left with the field edge and continue with the hedge on the left to the end of the field, passing to the left of a rather overgrown pond. Go through the gateway, and walk along the left-hand edge of the next field. After about 80 yards/73 m, and immediately after a small pond on the left, go through the gateway in front at the kink in the hedge. Continue along the right-hand edge of the following field.

Cross the roadway leading to Blackhales Farm, and then the fence. Turning left, walk along the left-hand edge of the field, passing the farm buildings on the left. Cross the fence at the corner of this field, and immediately passing to the left of a pond used as a rubbish dump, go through the small gap in the hedge just to the right of the hedge corner. Turning towards the right, walk across the narrower end of the field to the gateway a short distance in front. Go through this, and walk along the left-hand edge of the next field. Pass to the right of the pond at the end of this, and cross the ditch and fence into the following field. This appears to be the paddock or garden to the large new house across to the left. Walk straight ahead across this, and, passing some yards to the right of the garage, arrive at the intruding hedge corner coming from the right. Continue along the house driveway in front. Go through the gateway, with an RAC box opposite, and turning right walk along the main A452 road.

After approximately 75 yards/69 m, and just after the two buildings on the left, turn left through the gateway with a pond to its right. Walk along the left-hand edge of the field. Go through the gateway, and continue along the left-hand edge of the next one. Cross the fence and ditch, and turning left, walk along the left-hand edge of the following field. Cross the fence, and turning towards the right, walk diagonally across the next, heading towards the left-hand end of the farm buildings some way beyond. Cross the fence and ditch in front at the bottom of the field, a few yards to the left of the pond in the depression with the electricity power lines passing directly above it. Walk straight down the next field, keeping parallel to the power lines. Passing a few yards to the left of the pylon near the bottom of the field, arrive at an intruding corner coming from the left. Pass to the right of this, and continue alongside the hedge on the left. Cross the ditch and fence and, turning towards the right, walk diagonally up the following field, heading for the left-hand end of the barn at North Chase Farm. Cross the farm driveway, and continue to the corner just to the left of the barn. Cross the fence on the left of this corner, and turn right.

Extensive views are now seen. Across to the left, the spires of Coventry's churches are visible on the skyline. Kenilworth Castle is prominent in the middle distance.

Walk along the short right-hand top edge of the field, and after a few yards turn left in the corner, and continue with the hedge still on the right. After a short distance, where the hedge turns away to the right continue across the neck between the two parts of the field, to the intruding corner coming from the left. At this corner go through the gap in the hedge alongside the telegraph post. Walk diagonally across the field to the opposite far right-hand corner. Turn right through the gateway at the corner, and walk along the left-hand edge of the next field. After a few yards, where the hedge bears away to the left, continue straight ahead across the corner of the field, to the gateway directly in front. Go through this, and turning left walk along the left-hand edge of the next field, initially with a large pond on the left. Pass to the left of the barn at the corner, and immediately turn right and walk along the right-hand edge of the following field. Cross the field bridge over the stream, and go through the gateway. Continue ahead across the next field, heading for the intruding corner coming from the left. Cross the fence just to the left of this, and walk ahead up the right-hand edge of the following field. Pass through a group of young fir trees just to the right of a pond, and cross the stile at the corner. Turning right, walk up the right-hand edge of the next field. Kenilworth Castle is now very prominent across to the left.

At the top of the field, cross the fence, Chase Lane, and then the fence just to the right opposite. Turning towards the left, walk diagonally across the field, heading directly towards Kenilworth Castle some way ahead. From this fairly high ground, there are extensive views across to the right over the area that was once Kenilworth Great Pool. Cross the fence on the right of the field corner, and turning left walk along the left-hand edge of the next field. After a short distance, cross the fence at the corner, and walk ahead past a pond on the right. Immediately after this, turn towards the right, and walk

Kenilworth Castle

diagonally across the field, heading for the opposite corner, which is directly in line with the left-hand end of the Castle Keep beyond. This part of the route is waymarked with white-painted marks on the fence posts.

Cross the fence at the corner, and continue diagonally over the next field, now heading towards the right-hand end of the Castle ruins. Once the brow of the field has been crossed, the heading is between the brick farm building and the corrugated iron shed at the field corner. Pass immediately to the left of the iron shed, and go through the gateway in front into the corner of the next field. Continue diagonally across this, now heading approximately to the middle of the Castle ruins. Having crossed the brow of this field, continue down to the gateway on the right of the bottom corner. Go through this, and turning left walk along the track known as Purlieu Lane, crossing Finham Brook at the bottom of the slope. Continue up to where this track ends at Castle Road, with the picturesque cottages on Castle Green to the left and Kenilworth Castle on the right.

Kenilworth is one of the grandest ruined castles in England, with architectural styles ranging from Norman to Elizabethan. Built in mellow red sandstone, it now stands gaunt and open to the sky, dominated by the massive Keep.

Originally established by Geoffrey de Clinton around 1125, it was extended and altered by the monarchy up to Tudor times. Living quarters were added by John of Gaunt in the fourteenth century, which turned the former fortress into a medieval palace. Elizabeth I gave the Castle to her favourite, Robert Dudley, whom she created Earl of Leicester in 1564. This heralded the start of the most magnificent era in Kenilworth's existence, when costly and elaborate entertainments were arranged by Dudley for the Queen's pleasure during her visits. Partially destroyed during the Civil War, the Castle gradually became the ruin we see today.

Kenilworth perambulation

At the bottom of Castle Green, bear left past the Queen and

Church Green, Kenilworth
St Nicholas, Kenilworth

Castle Hotel and walk up Castle Hill, passing a good group of restored thatched-roof cottages on the right. From the top of the hill, continue along High Street. Abbey Fields drop down to the right, whilst the more modern part of the town can be seen across the valley. The parish church of St Nicholas, mainly Perpendicular in architectural feature but with a sumptuously decorated Norman doorway, is situated just behind the houses on the right, near the end of High Street.

At the crossroads at the foot of High Street, turn right down Bridge Street, and at the bottom of the slope just before the bridge, turn right along the footpath through the Abbey Fields. The ruins of St Mary's Abbey are shortly seen to the right of this path.

Originally founded as an Augustinian priory by Geoffrey de Clinton, who it has been noted also founded the Castle, St Mary's became an abbey in the fifteenth century. Very little now remains standing, and much of the old stonework can be seen in the wall supporting the terraces of St Nicholas's churchyard. The fourteenth-century gatehouse is partially intact, as is the nearby guesthouse.

Continuing on past the Abbey, pass the swimming pool on the left and, bearing right, walk alongside the brook. In season the low-lying area to the right often becomes flooded, forming a very attractive lake. Go through the gate at the end of the path, and turning right, walk along the road back to Castle Green.

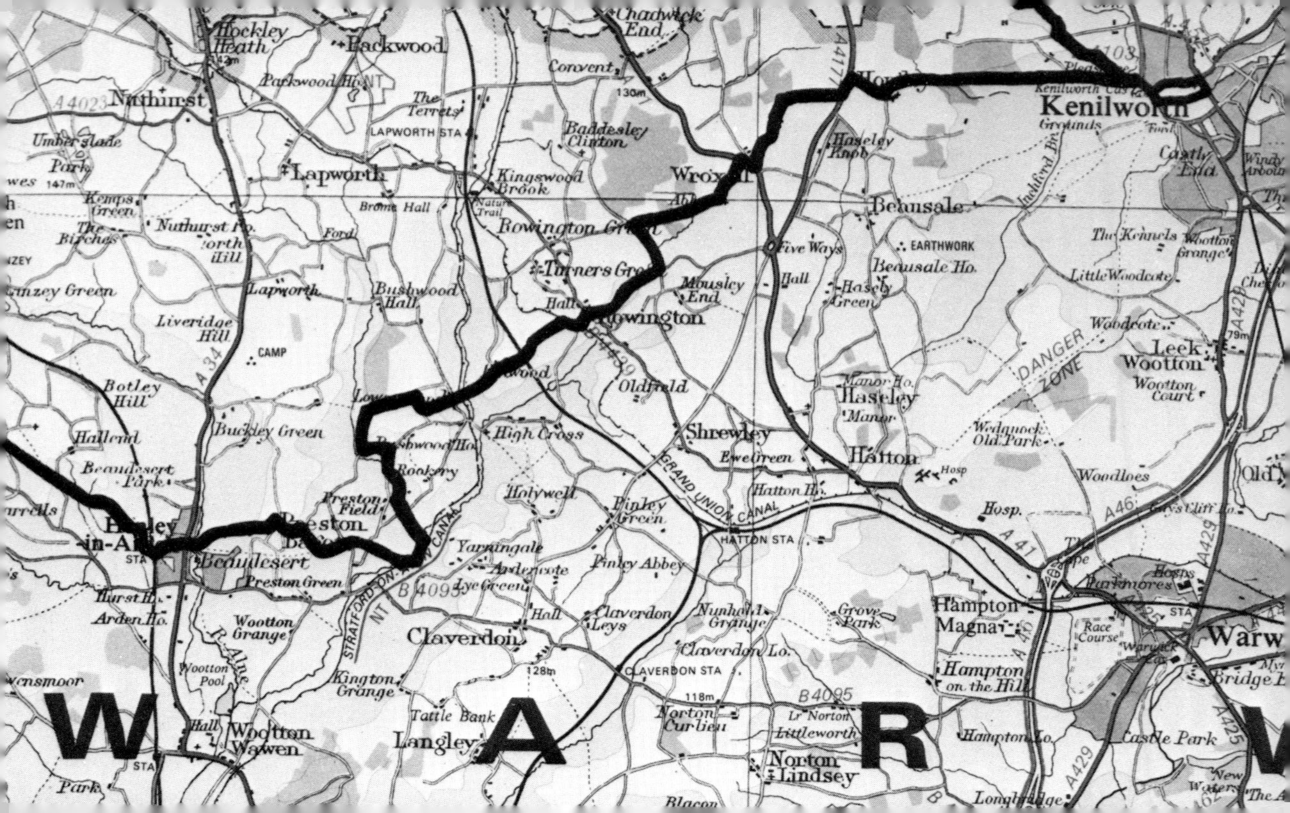

Kenilworth
Hockley Heath
Packwood
Nuthurst
Umberslade Park
Lapworth
LAPWORTH STA
Kingswood Brook
Baddesley Clinton
Convent
Wroxall
Haseley Knob
Beausale
EARTHWORK
Beausale Ho.
Five Ways
Rowington Green
Turners Green
Rowington
Mousley End
Oldfield
Shrewley
Haseley
Hatton
High Cross
Holywell
Pinley Green
Pinley Abbey
GRAND UNION CANAL
HATTON STA
Yarningale
Claverdon
CLAVERDON STA
Claverdon Leys
Nunhold Grange
Preston Green
Beaudesert
Wootton Wawen
Langley
Tattle Bank
Kington Grange
Norton Lindsey
Hampton Magna
Hampton on the Hill
Leek Wootton
Wootton Court
DANGER ZONE
Woodloes
Little Woodcote
The Kennels
Castle End
Warw
Race Course
Castle Park
Liveridge Hill
Botley Hill
Buckley Green
Bushwood Hall
Rookery
Preston Field
Wootton Grange
R. Alne
A4177
A34
A41
A46
A429
A425
B4095
B4439
A4023
W
A
R
W

2 **Kenilworth – Honiley – Wroxall – Rowington – Lowsonford – Preston Bagot – Henley in Arden**

Distance: 11 miles/17·7 km

From the Castle, retrace your steps down Purlieu Lane, recrossing Finham Brook at the bottom of the slope. Passing the field over which you previously walked, continue up the track. After some distance, pass High House Farm on the left, and continue along the less-well-used track in front, where the main track bears left into the farmyard. After a while the track finishes at a gate. Cross the stile alongside this, and walk straight across the field in front, heading directly for the pylon beyond. This heading leads you over the first part of the old earthwork in the field.

This earthwork, consisting of banks and ditches covering a large area, is known as The Pleasaunce. Rectangular in shape, with sides approximately 500 ft × 600 ft/152 m × 183 m, it was built by Henry V in about 1414 and carried a large timber-framed banqueting house. This was later used by visiting royalty for their state apartments, instead of those in Kenilworth Castle. It was demolished during the reign of Henry VIII.

Bearing left, pass to the left of the ditch surrounding the higher rectangular central area and, now heading some way to the left of the pylon, walk straight to the small gate on the right of the field corner. Passing through this, continue along the left-hand edge of the next field. Cross the stile, and walk along the right-hand edge of the following field. Cross another stile, and continue along the right-hand edge of the next field, alongside Chase Wood. Continue through the remains of a gateway, and walk along the right-hand edge of the following field, passing a pond which is just inside the edge of the wood. Continue straight on through the hedge at the end of this field, and along the right-hand edge of the one following. The spire of Honiley church is now seen across towards the left. Go through the gateway in front alongside the end of the wood, and continue along the right-hand edge of the next

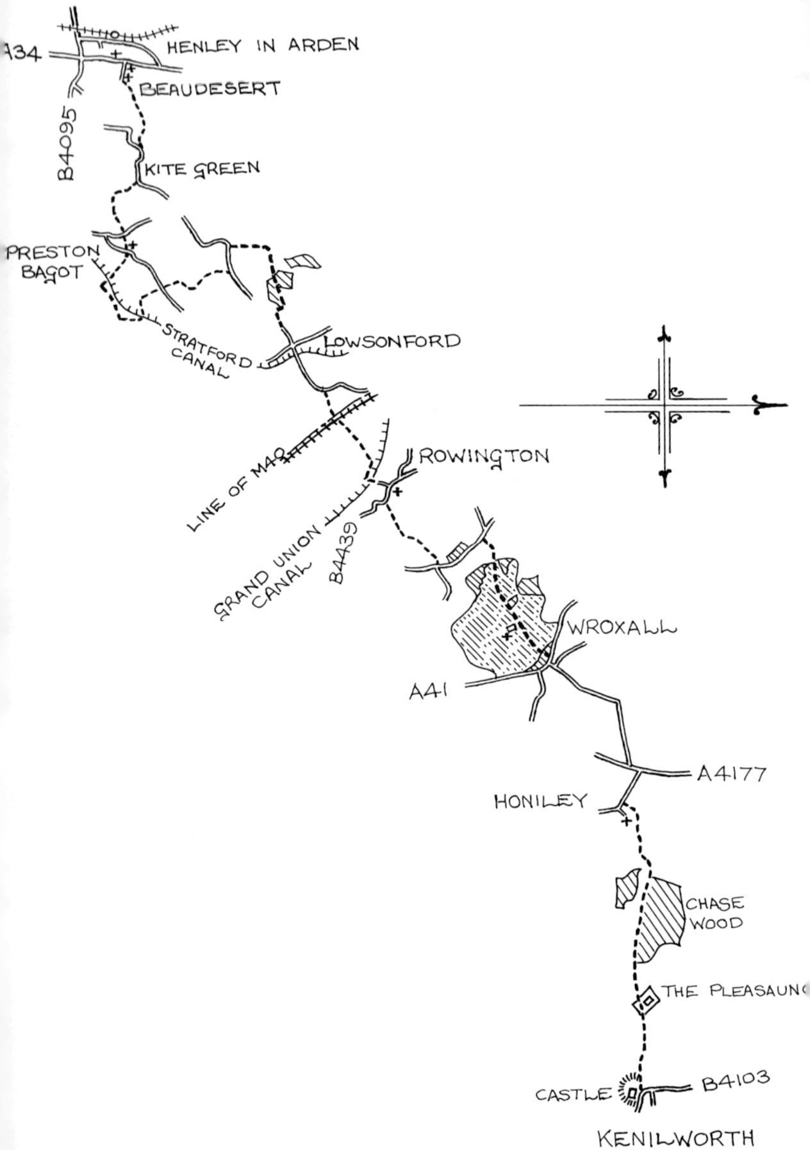

A34
HENLEY IN ARDEN
BEAUDESERT
B4095
KITE GREEN
PRESTON
BAGOT
STRATFORD
CANAL
LOWSONFORD
LINE OF M42
ROWINGTON
GRAND UNION
CANAL
B4439
WROXALL
A41
A4177
HONILEY
CHASE
WOOD
THE PLEASAUNC
CASTLE
B4103
KENILWORTH

Backward glance to Kenilworth Castle

field. Honiley Hall can be seen at the top of the rise in the field over to the left.

After about 200 yards/183 m, and about halfway along the field, bear left at the gateway on the right and walk diagonally across the field to the left-hand corner. This corner is not very obvious, and is located by heading just to the right of the loop in the stream and hedge on the left. Walk alongside this loop for a few yards, and then turn left through the gap in the hedge, just before an oak and then an ash tree. Cross the stream and climb the bank into the next field. Turning towards the right, walk straight across the field, keeping more or less parallel to the hedge which is about 50 yards/46 m over to the right, and heading for a point in that hedge which is seen just to the right of the solitary oak towards the far end of the field. Passing a few yards to the right of the oak, continue to the next oak at what is now seen as an intruding corner of the hedge. Cross the fence here, and continue along the left-hand edge of the next field. Cross the stile, and turning left, walk for a few yards along the left-hand edge of the following field. Pass through the fence and hedge in the corner, and walk straight across the next field to the small piece of fence in the hedge at the opposite side. Cross this on to the lane.

Your route turns right here, but a visit to Honiley church is a desirable diversion. To do this, turn left along the lane and, after a few yards, where the lane bends right, turn up the driveway on the left, leading to the church, the Malthouse, and the Lodges. (The driveway in front at the bend leads to Honiley Hall, which is now a Warwickshire County Council Residential Youth Centre.)

The driveway leads into a grassed courtyard, with a pond. The Lodges are to the right, and the Malthouse to the left, whilst directly in front the gateway in the wall leads to the tiny Baroque church of St John the Baptist. Built in 1723, it is reputed to have been designed by Sir Christopher Wren, who lived at nearby Wroxall Abbey.

Returning to the lane, turn right and proceed to its end at the main A4177 Stonebridge to Warwick link-road, opposite the Honiley Boot Inn. This dates from 1470 and is now picturesquely covered with virginia creeper. Turn left and walk along the main road for about 200 yards/183 m, and then turn right into the lane signposted *Wroxall*. Walk the full length of this pleasant lane—just over 1 mile/1·6 km—passing Manor Farm on the left; and arrive at the tiny village of Wroxall.

At the end of the lane, turn right along the main A41 road, and after approximately 100 yards/91 m turn through the Abbey gateway on the left between the stone pillars. Note the remains of the old stocks on the green to the right, opposite here. Walk along the driveway leading to Wroxall Abbey

St John the Baptist, Honiley

through the extensive parkland. After bearing gently right for some distance, the track now bears left, heading towards the walled garden which can be seen at the Abbey. Passing through the remains of a gateway at this point, cross an avenue of trees, and then immediately go through the iron kissing-gate in the fence on the right. Bearing slightly left, cross the parkland to the centre of the small copse. Go through the kissing gate, and crossing the copse, leave by another.

The nineteenth-century Abbey is now clearly visible in the trees to the left. Its predecessor was the home of Sir Christopher Wren, who purchased it in 1713.

Walk straight across the parkland heading for the centre of the Scots pine coppice seen beyond the field bottom. Having walked a few yards alongside a fence on the right, pass through the gate and over a stream. Bearing very slightly left, walk straight up the next field, passing some 60 yards/55 m to the right of the previously mentioned Scots pine coppice. Continue (heading some way to the right of the line of pines on the horizon), to the end of this very large field where it necks down and finishes at a point. (Ignore the small gate which is clearly seen in the hedge, a short distance to the left.) Cross the fence here, and walk ahead along the right-hand edge of the next field. Pass through the remains of a gateway, and turn left along the lane.

After about 600 yards/549 m, and having passed a narrow stretch of woodland on the right, turn right over the stile a few yards short of the lane junction, signposted *Five Ways* and *Coventry*. Proceed along the right-hand edge of the field. Cross the fence and ditch, and walk straight ahead across the field in front, to a point approximately one-third of the way across (about 125 yards/114 m) keeping parallel to the bottom right-hand edge. Bear towards the right here, and walk diagonally down the field to the large willow tree seen in the bottom edge (just to the left of the tower of Rowington church on the hill beyond). Cross the stream and fence just to the right of this tree, (a little further to the left along the edge of the field from this point, the field-bridge over the stream, useful when the stream is in flood, is unfortunately not on the definitive route). Turning towards the left continue diagonally across the next field still heading a short way to the left of the church tower. Cross the stile immediately on the right of the intruding corner coming down from the right, and walk along the short left-hand bottom edge of the following field. Cross the stile alongside the gate, and bearing towards the right walk diagonally up the next field to its top left-hand corner. Cross the stile here and walk up the left hand edge of the churchyard above the B4439 road.

The church of St Lawrence, Rowington, is a mixture of architectural styles, from the Norman north wall to the Perpendicular west doorway and five-light window. The tower over the nave crossing was built about 1300.

Turn left down the steps outside the south doorway of the church, and then turning right walk for a few yards up the B4439 road, to turn left along the narrow tarmac roadway at the right hand bend, noting the old iron 'milestone' set in a modern wall. Follow this roadway, and shortly cross over the Grand Union Canal. Immediately after the bridge, turn through the gateway on the right and walk along the right-hand edge of the field, above the canal in its very deep cutting. Bear left at the first corner in the field, and continue following the right-hand edge.

Railway sleepers are evident along this section of the path, as they are for the next ½-mile/800 m, although a little obscure in places. These were apparently laid years ago to make it easier for schoolchildren to walk from Lowsonford to Rowington, on their journey to and from school each day. Because of this, the footpath is known locally as the Sleeper Path.

At the end of the field, the Sleeper Path continues straight across a rather rickety wooden bridge over a pond, but by deviating to the left you can walk round the edge of this pond. Go through the gateway in front, and continue along the right-hand edge of the next field. Shrewley village can be seen some distance away, across to the left. At the end of the field the path continues straight on over a railway bridge. This bridge, numbered 173, crosses the main London–Birmingham railway-line.

The projected line of the M40 motorway runs in the cutting alongside the railway at this point, and if it is constructed the present bridge will be demolished and replaced by a new one, parallel to it and about 50 ft/15 m to the left. This new bridge will span both railway and road. On each bank of the cutting, a short section of new path will link the existing path to the new bridge, and this will constitute a modification to the direction given in the preceding paragraph.

Go through the gateway at the end of the bridge, and (sleepers still in evidence) continue along the fenced and hedged track. A few yards before reaching a gate across the track, go through the small gate to the left and continue along the narrow fenced and hedged path running parallel to the track. Presently go through the small gate across this path, and continue to the gate leading on to the lane, and passing Finwood Farm on the right. Turn left along the lane.

The countryside in this area is fairly well wooded, and is of a gently undulating nature. Fields are both arable and pasture.

Walk along the lane and, gradually dropping downhill, cross the Stratford-on-Avon Canal into Lowsonford village. At the major road, note the old village pump on the right, set in paving slabs. A short distance along to the left is the Fleur de Lys Inn. Your route crosses straight over the major road, and continues along the narrow lane opposite. Walk along this, climbing gently uphill. Where the lane bends sharply to the left, and opposite a cottage, cross the stile on the right. Walk along the right-hand edge of the small field, alongside the line of elm stumps. Go through the gateway, and continue straight across the next field to its far left-hand corner, passing to the right of the intruding corner. Note the embankment on the right as you cross this field; it once carried the Birmingham–Henley-in-Arden railway.

Cross the fence and walk ahead up the next field to the left-hand end of the old railway bridge, which now has its arch filled in. Go through the gateway at this point and, turning right, cross the bridge and walk for a few yards along the short track to the end of the fir plantation on the left. Turn through the gateway on the left here, and walk up the left-hand edge of the field, alongside the plantation. Cross the fence, and continue straight ahead along the firebreak track running through the plantation. This track descends fairly steeply.

At the end of the plantation, walk straight ahead to the gateway in the hedge on the left, where you join a track coming down from the right. Turn left through this gateway,

Lock and bridge. Stratford on Avon Canal

and follow the well defined track which bears round to the right. Where this track nears the hedge on the left, beyond which is the line of the old railway, continue straight on along the left-hand edge of the field. Cross the fence at the corner of this field, and turn left along the farm roadway leading from Coppice Corner Farm across to the right. Immediately, cross the bridge over the old railway and follow the tarmac roadway to the lane, noting the pleasant views all around.

Turn left and walk along the lane for approximately a $\frac{1}{4}$-mile/400 m, and then turn sharp right on to the hedged track alongside the entrance to Willowbrook House. Follow this, and shortly cross the footbridge alongside the ford. Follow the path beside the ford for a few yards, and then turn through the gateway on the left. Walk along the left-hand edge of the field, following the stream. Cross the stile, and continue across the next field to the stile which can be seen in the hedge in front. Cross the footbridge over a small stream just before reaching this stile and then, crosssing the stile, walk ahead in the next field to the bank of the stream. Where the stream loops away to the left, continue straight on across the field, following the line of old tree-stumps to the point where the stream returns again. From this point, continue along the edge of the stream. Pass through the hedge, and follow the stream along the edge of the next field.

Cross the fence and then the lane, and, passing through the gateway in front, walk along the left-hand edge of the field, again following the stream. Go through the gateway, and continue beside the stream along the edge of the following field. At the end of this field, turn through the gateway leading into the left-hand of the two fields immediately in front. Walk along the left-hand edge of this field, still following the stream. The whole of this section beside the stream has been through a very pleasant vale, with well-wooded pastures all around.

Pass through the gateway at the end of the field, and cross the old brick bridge over the stream. Walk along the left-hand edge of the small field to the gateway. Go through this, on to the towing path of the Stratford-on-Avon Canal, which belongs to the National Trust. Immediately cross the cast-iron bridge in front alongside lock number 35. This bridge, numbered 45, is unusual, being slotted through its centre which allowed the towing rope of the old horse-drawn narrow-boats to pass through. Go through the gateway in front, and turning towards the right, walk diagonally across the field to the far left-hand corner. (At times the first part of this field can be rather boggy, and if desired an alternative route is to return to the towing path and to walk along it in the same direction as the field path, picking up the main route where it recrosses the canal.)

Go through the gateway in the corner, and turning towards

Old barn, near Preston Bagot

the right walk diagonally across the next field to its far right-hand corner, alongside the canal. Cross a brook, and walk beside the canal. Cross the fence, and continue along the right-hand edge of the following field. Near the end of this, arrive at lock number 36. At the end of this lock, go through the gateway and, turning right, cross another slotted cast-iron bridge over the canal, noting the unusual barrel-roofed cottage at the next lock. (At this point those who have followed the alternative route along the towing path, now rejoin the main route.)

Walk straight ahead along the track and, shortly crossing a bridge over a stream, arrive at the end of the track. Cross the stile alongside the left-hand of the two gates, and turning towards the right, walk diagonally up the field to the far left-hand corner, with a barn seen to its right and Preston Bagot church beyond. Some way up the field, your diagonal brings you alongside the left-hand fence, which you follow to the corner. Pass through the gateway in this corner and, bearing slightly to the left, walk up the next field to the stile in the hedge in front. From this point at the top of the field, excellent views are seen looking back over the direction from which you have come.

Cross the stile, and the lane, and go through the gateway opposite, immediately to the left of the churchyard. Walk alongside this, passing the mainly Norman church of All Saints, with its timber bell-turret. The view from here encompasses well over 180 degrees. Continue along the footpath to the gateway in front. Pass through this, and descend the steep, narrow, hedged path.

At the bottom of the slope, cross the lane and the stile opposite, alongside Church Farm. Walk along the right-hand edge of the field. Cross the stile and a ditch, and walk ahead over the small field. At the hedge, cross the stile leading into the left-hand of the two fields immediately in front. Walk along the right-hand edge of this, and cross a further stile. Continue straight over the next field, to the prominent tree which can be seen in the far hedge directly in front. Cross the fence on the right of this tree into the corner of the next field. Immediately turn right, and cross the next fence into the following field. Walk along the right-hand edge of this and, nearing its end, turn through the gateway on the right before reaching the house. Walk along the short track to the lane.

Turn left and walk along the lane, following it round a sharp right-hand bend and passing a lane leading off to the left. You are now in the hamlet of Kite Green. Pass a lane on your right, opposite a bungalow named The Nest, and just past here where your lane bends left, cross the stile on the right opposite a small pond. Turn towards the left, and walk diagonally across the field to the end of the line of trees running up from the corner. Cross the fence, and turning right in the corner of the next field, walk along its right-hand edge. Cross the fence, and turning towards the left, follow the well defined footpath which runs diagonally downhill towards Beaudesert Mount which is seen in front. Note Henley-in-Arden in the valley beyond the Mount, and the far-reaching views to the west. At the bottom of the slope pass through the line of hawthorn bushes, and continue up the hill in front towards the top of the Mount. Just below the summit, the path runs along the top of the earth rampart which curves around the right-hand side of the actual summit platform, but a detour to the top is well worthwhile, to view the magnificent panorama.

The Mount is all that now remains of the de Montfort castle, the earthworks dating from the eleventh century.

After skirting the summit continue ahead, still on the higher ground, keeping above the line of bushes on the right. Drop steeply down the slope to the gate leading on to the road alongside Beaudesert churchyard.

The church of St Nicholas is a good example of a Warwickshire Norman church. The chancel is completely of this period, as are the fine north and south doorways. The west tower is Perpendicular.

Turn right, and walk for a short distance along the road into the centre of Henley-in-Arden, crossing the little River

South doorway, St Nicholas, Beaudesert

Henley-in-Arden, St John the Baptist and Guildhall

Alne on the way.

Arriving at the main A34 road through the town, the parish church of St John the Baptist is immediately on the right. This is fifteenth century, as is the timbered Guildhall next door, built in 1448 by Ralph Boteler whose arms are over the fireplace.

Turn right, and walk along the main road for a short distance to the fifteenth-century market cross, set in its bed of cobblestones at the town centre.

Henley-in-Arden is basically one long main street running from north to south, and this is lined with delightful buildings of all styles and periods. There are several inns from which to choose when in search of refreshment.

Market Cross, Henley-in-Arden

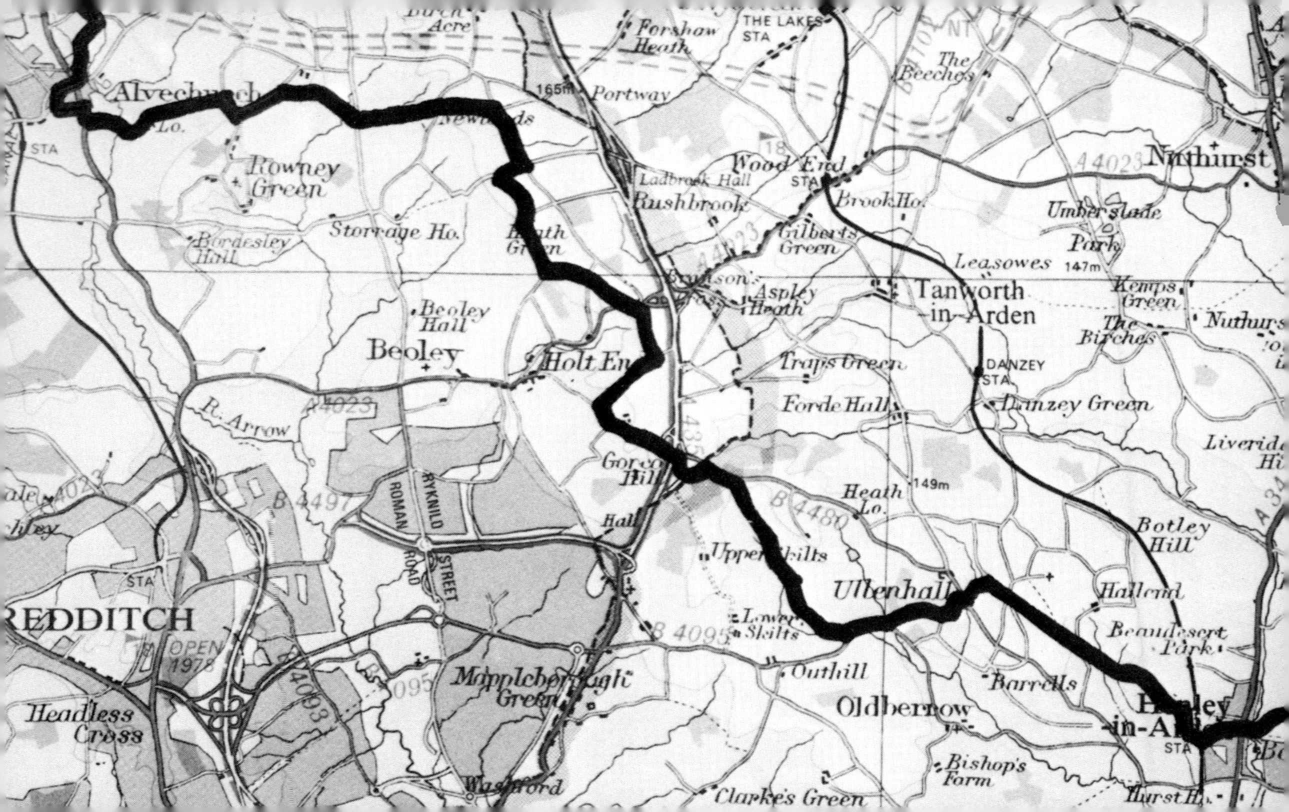
Forshaw Heath
THE LAKES STA
The Beeches
Portway
165m
Rowney Green
Storrage Ho.
Bordesley Hall
Wood End STA
Ladbrook Hall
Rushbrook
Brook Ho.
Umberslade Park
Gilberts Green
Leasowes
147m
A 4023
Nuthurst
Aspley Heath
Tanworth in-Arden
Kemps Green
The Birches
Beoley Hall
Beoley
Holt End
Trapps Green
DANZEY STA
Danzey Green
Forde Hall
R. Arrow
Gorcott Hill
RYKNILD STREET
ROMAN ROAD
Heath Lo.
149m
B 4480
Botley Hill
Upper Skilts
Ullenhall
Hallend
Lower Skilts
B 4095
Beaudesert Park
REDDITCH
OPEN 1978
Outhill
Barrells
Headless Cross
B 4093
Oldberrow
Bishop's Farm
Clarke's Green
Hurst Ho.
STA

3 **Henley in Arden – Ullenhall – Alvechurch**

Distance: 10¼ miles/16.5 km

From the old market cross in the centre of Henley-in-Arden, walk along the main A34 road towards the Guildhall and Parish Church, retracing your earlier steps. After a few yards, turn right into the narrow roadway opposite the chemist's shop and running alongside the auctioneers' office. Follow this and crossing the car park at the end, continue up the concrete path to the top of the incline. Pass through the gateway on to the road, and turning left walk along this for a few yards. Turn right, and cross the footbridge over the railway and station. Immediately over this bridge, turn sharp right, and walk along the right-hand edge of the allotment field. Cross the stile, and proceed along the right-hand edge of the field, and shortly continue along the narrow fenced section to the next stile. Cross this and, turning left, walk for a few yards along the track to the gateway in front. Pass through this into a very large field. Turn slightly towards the right and note the gateway that can be seen in the far hedge, in line with the electricity pylon some way beyond. Your objective is this gateway.

Initially, turn further towards the right and walk straight across the field towards the clump of trees and bushes in the centre which conceal a pond. Pass about 10 yards/9 m to the left of this and, turning slightly towards the left, continue ahead directly to the gateway. Go through this, and walk straight across the next field to the stile in the hedge. Cross this, and again continue straight ahead over the following field, heading towards the opening that can be seen between the two trees on the skyline and some way to the left of the pylon that can still be seen beyond. Once the brow of the field has been crossed, the gateway can be clearly seen ahead. Pass through this, and walk straight across the next field, heading towards a tree, with a gap in the far hedge just to the right of it (this is about one-third of the way between the two pylons seen beyond).

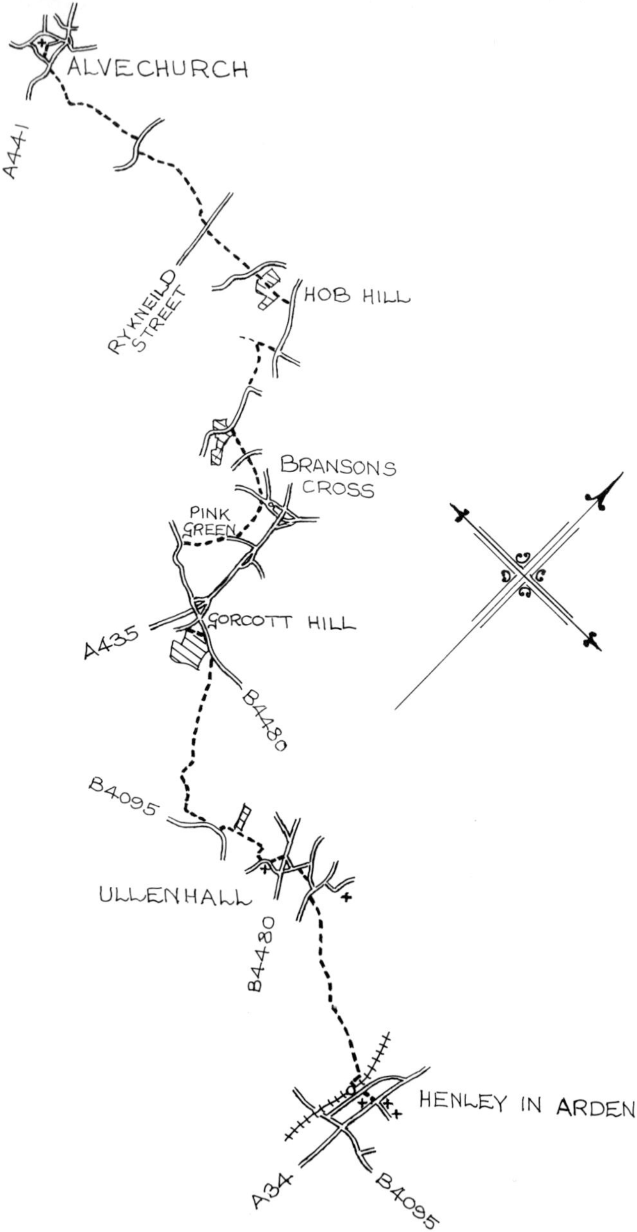
ALVECHURCH
A441
RYKNEILD STREET
HOB HILL
BRANSONS CROSS
PINK GREEN
GORCOTT HILL
A435
B4480
B4095
ULLENHALL
B4480
HENLEY IN ARDEN
A34
B4095

A short way before the hedge, pass to the right of the tree in the field, and continue to the stile in front, leading into the right-hand of the two fields beyond. Cross this and a small stream, and, turning towards the right, walk diagonally across the bottom end of this field to the stile which can be seen in front. Cross this, and then the plank footbridge over another stream, and continue across the next field to the intruding hedge corner coming from the left, some way in front. On nearing this, a pond is seen to its left. At this intruding corner, cross a track, and continue in the same direction across the remainder of the field, heading between a gate in the hedge to the left and a clump of trees and bushes to the right. Arriving between the gate and clump, a stile can be seen directly ahead, immediately to the right of two oak trees. Amongst the clump of trees, the pond is much favoured by mallard.

Cross the stile, and continue diagonally to the right across the following field, to the gateway which is seen just to the left of the house beyond. Note the old St Mary's church, Ullenhall, which is on the low rise across towards the right. Cross the stile alongside the gateway, and walk straight across the next field to the stile leading into the right-hand of the two fields beyond. Cross this, and walk along the left-hand edge of the field, shortly passing to the left of a pond. Continue to the corner, and crossing the stile, walk straight across the following small field to the gateway in front, passing to the left of another pond.

Go through the gateway, and turning right walk along the lane for a few yards, and then turn first left into the lane signposted *Ullenhall ½ mile/800 m*, noting the unusual gate on the left. Follow this lane for approximately 200 yards/183 m to the end of the second field on the left. Turn left here, through the small gate into the third field, and walk along the well defined footpath across it. Good evidence of the old ridge-and-furrow system of farming is to be seen in this field. At the end of the field, turn left round the end of the farm building and go through the small gate in front. Continue along the raised footpath beside the lane. At the end of this, turn right along the short lane into the centre of Ullenhall village.

Pass the war memorial, and bear right for a few yards along the main B4480 road through the village, passing the Post Office on the right. Immediately before reaching the Winged Spur Inn, cross the road and turn left along the narrow tarmac footpath at the left of Ullenhall Garage. Proceed along this and, shortly passing through a kissing-gate, follow the footpath across a field towards Ullenhall church. Go through the gate opposite the church of St Mary, built in 1875, and turn right along the lane.

Walk along this for a few yards, and turn through the first gateway on the right at the left-hand bend. Walk ahead across

Ullenhall Village

the field, following the well defined track leading to the house called Chapel Barn. Just before reaching the gate in front of the house, bear right and walk across the field corner to the stile in the hedge in front. Cross this, and follow the narrow path through the double hedge to a second stile. Cross this and, turning left, walk along the left-hand edge of the field. Go through the gateway and walk along the right-hand edge of the small field. At the corner of this, cross the fence in front and continue along the right-hand edge of the next field. The countryside in this area is pleasantly undulating and well wooded. Pass through the gateway, and walk along the right-hand edge of the next field. Go through the gateway at the end of this field, and walk straight ahead across the one

St. Mary's, Ullenhall

following, to its far left-hand corner. In doing this, initially walk alongside the end of the wood on the right, and shortly continue along the field's left-hand edge. At the corner cross the fence and ditch and, turning towards the left, cross a stream; immediately passing through a line of bushes and trees, walk straight across the next field to the gateway that can be seen in front of the barn at Tracy Farm.

Pass through the gateway, and turning right, walk along the main B4095 road. A few yards after passing the first cottage on the right, and at a point where the road bends to the left, turn right and cross the fence immediately on the left of a gateway. Walk diagonally across the field to a point about halfway along its right-hand edge, and then continue along this edge to the corner. Cross the fence and ditch and, turning right, walk along the right-hand edge of the next field. In following the edge of this field, first walk alongside the stream on the right for a few yards, and, crossing it where it bends left, ascend gently and pass to the right of a pond. A few yards after this, still following the right-hand edge, pass to the right of a farm building, and continue alongside a line of oak trees on the left to the end of the field.

Cross the fence, and walk along the right-hand edge of the next field. Just before the corner of this, bear left and cross the fence and hedge in front, at a point some 15 yards/14 m to the left of the corner. Walk ahead along the right-hand edge of the following field. The path ascends gently, and extensive views gradually appear to the right and behind. Go through the gateway, and continue along the right-hand edge of the next field, passing a pond on the left in a rather deep depression just after the gate. Go through the gateway at the end of this field, and continue along the right-hand edge of the one following. Pass through the gateway at the end of this, and walk straight on along the right-hand edge of the next one. Cross the fence in the corner of this field and, now climbing more steeply, follow the right-hand edge of the next one. Continue through the hedge in front, and walk along the right-hand edge of the following field. Cross the fence in the corner of this, and continue along the right-hand end of a narrow field. Cross the fence, and walk along the right-hand edge of the garden of a very large bungalow. Cross the stile at the front of the garden on to the main B4480 road.

Turn left along the road, and shortly after passing the row of cottages on the left with a wood behind them, turn left over the stile and walk along the left-hand edge of the field, alongside the wood. The ditch along the right-hand side of this field is the source of the River Alne, which you crossed earlier in Henley-in-Arden. Go through the gateway in the corner of the field on to the old road. Just to the left at this point is the top of Gorcott Hill, and a few yards down this bypassed and very quiet road is the Holly Bush Inn. There are good views from the top of the hill.

Turn right and walk along the road; and at its end turn left along the B4480 road, crossing the bridge over the dual carriageway A435 Birmingham–Alcester road. Immediately after this bridge, turn left along the lane signposted *Beoley*. Walk along this lane, noting the views to the left over Redditch New Town and, where the lane descends steeply, the excellent view in front, extending from the Lickeys in the north to the Malverns in the south, with Rowney Green village some way in front. At the foot of this steep descent, pass a farm on the right at a sharp left-hand bend; and then following the lane, bear round to the right, passing the entrance to Lower Greenhills Farm at the next bend. Approximately 200 yards/183 m past this, and having passed through a shallow cutting, turn through the gateway on the right where the lane again bends left.

Climb straight up the fairly steep field in front, heading just to the left of the tree-lined depression towards the field brow. Arriving at the top of the depression, bear very slightly towards the left, and still ascending, continue alongside the hedge on the right, heading just to the right of the house at Pink Green in front at the top of the hill. Passing through the gateway, turn right and immediately left, and walk along the left-hand edge of the field past the front of the house garden.

At the end of this, go through the gate on the left and, turning right, walk along the rough lane.

About 40 yards/37 m before reaching the house and cottage—shortly before the lane ends at the main A435 road—turn across the fence on the left and walk ahead along the right-hand edge of the field. Cross the fence at the first corner and, bearing towards the right, walk straight across the next field to the gateway at the far side, just beyond the pond. In crossing this field, pass to the left of the pond. Go through the gateway and proceed straight across the next field, keeping parallel to its right-hand edge and heading towards the silo at the farm ahead. Cross the fence, and continue across the following field to the gateway just to the left of the farm complex. Pass through the double gateway across the end of the farmyard, and walk straight across the field in front to the telegraph pole at the far side. This is just to the right of the point where the fence in front changes to the established hedge.

Cross the fence, the main A4023 Coventry–Redditch road, and the fence directly opposite. Turning towards the left, walk diagonally across the field to the gateway in the far hedge. Go through this, and walk straight across the next field to the stile in the far hedge. (This is located by heading directly towards the poplar trees seen just to the right of the house beyond.) Cross the stile, and walk ahead along the fenced and hedged path. Passing the house and its outbuildings, arrive at the end of this narrow section. Cross the stile in front, and bear left along the lane. Almost immediately turn across the stile on the right, and walk along the left-hand edge of the field. Cross the fence, and continue along the left-hand edge of the next one.

Cross the stile at the end of the field, and turn right along the lane. Good views are seen across to the left. After approximately 600 yards/549 m, where the lane bends sharply to the right continue ahead along the track in front. At the end of this, where it forks to join a cross-track, take the right-hand fork; and then, turning right, walk along the cross-track.

At the end of this track, turn left along the lane. After approximately 400 yards/366 m pass a lane on the left; and then after another 250 yards/229 m and alongside the second field on the left from the lane, turn through the gateway on the left into this field (not the second gateway at the end of the field, just before Hobhill Farm). Walk diagonally to the right across the corner of the field, to the point where the right-hand hedge turns away to the right. Continue straight ahead from this point, still following the diagonal, and cross the fence in front. Walk across the next field, following the same line, to the point in front where the right-hand hedge bears away to the right. Cross a farm track here, and continue ahead alongside the hedge on the right. After a few yards, the hedge turns slightly more towards the right, but your route continues straight ahead to the far side of the field, in line with the trigonometrical point on the brow of the field beyond. Cross the fence and walk across the next field to this trigonometrical point on the summit of Hob Hill. Go on, and walk down the slope, passing between the end few trees of the woodland. Extensive views are now seen from the Lickey Hills to the right, to Redditch to the left, and with Rowney Green across the valley in front. Continue straight downhill to the stile at the bottom of the field, which can be seen just to the right of the house on the opposite side of the lane.

Cross the stile and the lane, and go through the gateway opposite. Walk straight across the field to the left-hand of the two gates which are seen in front, with a Dutch barn in line beyond. Pass through this gateway and walk along the right-hand edge of the small field. Passing to the right of the farm complex, cross the fence in the corner of this field. Initially walk for a few yards along the right-hand edge of the next, very large field; and then, bearing slightly towards the left, follow the fairly well defined track to the gateway at the intruding corner coming from the left some way ahead, and heading towards Rowney Green village on its hill. Note the stump of an old windmill on the top of Weatheroak Hill, across to the right. Pass through the gateway and walk along the right-hand edge of the next field.

Go through the gateway in the corner of the field, and turn right along the narrow Roman Ryknield Street. Almost immediately, and having crossed a brook, turn left across the stile into the corner of the field. Walk along the left-hand edge of this, and at the end, cross the footbridge over a stream. Walk ahead for a few yards across the next field and then, bearing right, walk gently uphill along its left-hand edge. At the top of this field, cross a temporary fence and then shortly the fence in front at the corner, with a depression just to the right; and turning slightly towards the left, walk straight across the next field to its top left-hand corner. In crossing this field, pass immediately to the left of a second depression, noting the good long view across to the left towards Redditch. Cross the fence in front, just to the right of the corner; and continuing over the narrow neck at the left-hand end of the next field, cross the fence directly in front into the corner of the following field.

The Lickey Hills are now seen in front. Turning slightly towards the left, walk diagonally across the field, heading towards the left-hand end of the clump of trees a short way in front, just over the brow of the field. Cross the fence in front, just to the left of the clump (which it will now be seen surrounds a depression), into the corner of the next field. Following the same diagonal, continue downhill to the opposite corner, initially passing to the left of another depression. Turn through the gateway on the left of the corner, and walk along the fairly good track, following the right-hand edge of the next field. After a short distance cross a small stream, and continue along the now-fenced track. Pass through the gateway near the top of the climb, with Rowney Green House Farm on the right, and continue along the track which now becomes the driveway of the farm.

At the end of the driveway turn right down the lane, and after about 150 yards/137 m, pass Rose Cottage at a right-hand bend. After approximately 80 more yards/73 m, turn through the gateway on the left into the entrance to Rowney

Lodge Farm. Walk ahead along the track, passing the farm buildings on the right. Continue through the gateway in front and along the right hand-edge of the field, following the same track. Pass through the gateway at the end of the field, and continue along the right-hand edge of the next one. An excellent view of the Lickey Hills is seen across to the right, and Alvechurch village is now in sight down in the valley in front. Pass a pond in a depression on the left. Go through the gateway at the end of the field and, passing Alvechurch Lodge on the left, walk along the hedged track. This shortly continues as a tarmac roadway running fairly steeply downhill. At the foot of the hill cross the River Arrow, and continue to the end of the roadway, which now reverts to a track.

St Laurence, Alvechurch

Cross the cattle-grid and, passing through the iron gateway, turn right along the main A441 road at the entrance to Alvechurch village. After a few yards turn left up School Lane; and in approximately 100 yards/91 m turn right opposite St Mary's RC church, and walk along the hedged and fenced tarmac footpath on the right of the Rectory garden. Go through the iron kissing-gate, and continue along the path in St Laurence churchyard. After a few yards, join the main path leading up to St Laurence church. This was rebuilt in the nineteenth century, but it has much remaining from earlier periods. The south doorway is Norman, and the tower is seventeenth century.

The Old House, Alvechurch

From the point where we joined the main path up to the church, turn right through the gateway and out of the churchyard. Walk down the hedged tarmac roadway in front and, bearing right at the bottom of this at the small triangular village green, continue down Bear Hill to the main road at the bottom, with the village square opposite. The Swan Inn is a short way along to the right.

Hagley Park
Hall
Clent Grove
Clent Hills
Walton Hill
Adams Hill
Clent
Holy Cross
Walton Ho.
Moor Hall
The Grange
Belbroughton Lo.
Yewtree Ho.
Bell Hall
Hartle
Belbroughton
Bradford Ho.
Broom Hill
Fairfield Co.
Fairfield
Wildmoor
Bell End
Castle Bourne
Bell Heath
NT
Great Farley Wood
283m
165m
A 491
B4551
Hunnington
B45
Romsley
M5
Gannow Green
Country Park
Frankley Green
Frankley
Frankley Beeches
Frankley Resr.
Hosp.
Rubery
Eachway
Lickey
Lydiate Ash
Marlbrook
Lickey Grange
Upper Catshill
Catshill
Staple Hill
Lickey End
Bourneath
Dordale
Worms Ash
Bromsgrove
Dodford
A 448
A38
M42
4
Linthurst
Northfield
A38
Longbridge
Turves Green
Cofton Common
Grovely Ho.
Rednal
Cofton Hackett
Country Park
Kendal End
Upper Bittell Resr.
Barnt Green
BARNT GREEN STA
Uplands
Withybed Green
STA
Alvechurch
Lo.
Arrowfield Top
Lower Bittell Resr.
The Leys
Moorgreen Hall
Lea End
Hopwood
Grovely Dingle
Forhill
Tunnel
Hawkesley Hall
Headley Heath
West Heath
King's Norton
Walker's Heath
Cotteridge
White Hill
B4121
A4123
A441
Weat

4 Alvechurch – Cofton Hackett – Lickey Hills – Clent Hills – Adams Hill

Distance: $11\frac{3}{4}$ miles/19 km

Leaving the village square of Alvechurch, walk along Red Lion Street, the main A441 Birmingham road. After a short distance, turn right into Meadow Lane opposite the Red Lion Inn. Walk the length of this, and pass through the iron gates into the Alvechurch playing-field. Immediately turn left along the path running between the double line of trees, and after a few yards cross a small stream. Continue along the path, which shortly bears right and runs across the end of the playing-field to the corner. Pass through the iron kissing-gate here, and walk along the left-hand edge of the field. At the end of this, continue along the short hedged track and through the gateway.

Turn left and walk along the lane. A short way along this, pass alongside a mill stream and then, at the left-hand bend, cross the stile in front to the right of Arrow Cottage. Continue along the path between the mill stream and a fence. Cross the stile at the end of this, and walk along the right-hand side of the field beside the River Arrow.

The projected line of the M42 motorway crosses this field, and if built, will be carried on a bridge over both river and footpath.

Near the end of the field, continue across its neck to the stile in the hedge in front. Cross this, and turning left walk along the lane.

At the end of the lane continue straight across the main A441 road at the roundabout, and walk along the B4120 road opposite, signposted *Barnt Green*. After about 400 yards/366 m, where the road turns sharply left, cross the stile on the right, alongside Little Stannalls, and follow the footpath signposted *Upper Bittell Reservoir*. For a few yards this path runs through bushes, before crossing the footbridge over the River Arrow. From the footbridge, walk across the field, heading initially towards Bittell Farm which is seen on top of the rise in front. Approximately two-thirds of the way across

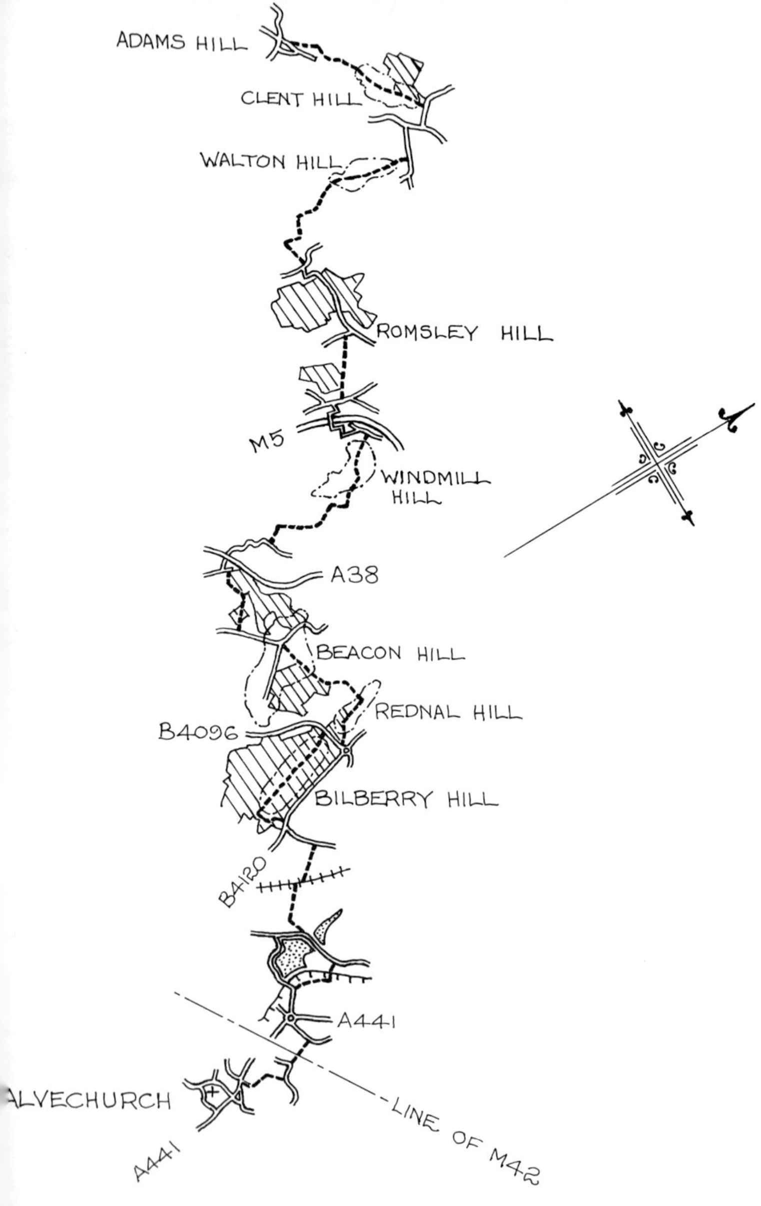
ADAMS HILL
CLENT HILL
WALTON HILL
ROMSLEY HILL
M5
WINDMILL HILL
A38
BEACON HILL
REDNAL HILL
B4096
BILBERRY HILL
B4120
A441
ALVECHURCH
A441
LINE OF M42

Worcester and Birmingham Canal, near Bittell

the field, bear towards the right, and walk to the bridge that can be seen spanning the Worcester and Birmingham Canal at the top corner of the field. Passing through the gateway, cross the bridge and walk up the fenced track in front. Go through the gateway and, crossing the farmyard at Bittell Farm, turn right through the sheet steel gates. Follow the concrete roadway and, passing through the gateway between the bungalow and a pond, continue to the road.

Turn left and walk along the road, which shortly descends to run between the two sections of Lower Bittell Reservoir. Immediately past the reservoir, where the road bends left, continue straight ahead through the gateway in front, into the corner of the field. Walk ahead diagonally across this to its far corner, passing to the left of the pond in the middle. Cross the stile in the corner and turn right. Immediately go through the gateway in front, and walk along the right-hand edge of the following field. The path now gradually climbs, and affords good views across to the right over the Bittell Reservoirs. Arriving at the field corner (immediately before reaching a pond in a tree-lined depression), cross the fence on the right and continue along the left-hand edge of the adjacent field. Cross the stile in front and climb the embankment on to the main Birmingham–Bristol railway-line. Cross the tracks to the next stile at the foot of the opposite side of the embankment, about 85 yards/78 m diagonally to the right. Cross this stile, and then immediately the fence on the right, into the corner of the field. Turning slightly towards the left, walk diagonally across the field, heading approximately midway between Cofton Hall to the right and the end of the line of houses across to the left. Cross the fence at the far edge of the field, and continue across the next field to the gateway seen a short distance to the left of the stretch of woodland. Go through this gateway, and turn left along the lane into Cofton Hackett.

Climb gently towards the Lickey Hills in front, and at the end of the lane turn right along the main B4120 road. After a few yards, turn through the gateway on the left into the woodland at the foot of the Lickey Hills.

Gradually climbing, follow the good track, which at first bears left and then shortly right. Where this turns more sharply to the right, turn right, and climb the path leading steeply up Cofton Hill, past a fenced depression on the right. Upon reaching a cross-track, bear left and follow this, now climbing less steeply. Scots pines and silver birch predominate on this well-wooded hill. After crossing the summit, the track bears slightly to the left, and begins a gradual descent. At this point, bear towards the right and follow the path along the summit ridge. Views to the right are now extensive over the outskirts of Birmingham. After gradually descending, the path continues down a flight of steps cut from the hillside, dropping steeply to the road at the bottom.

Turn right, and walk along the main B4096 road. Just before reaching the roundabout at Rednal and immediately after passing the Bilberry Hill Training Centre on the right, turn left and climb the steps up Rednal Hill. Once again, climb steeply, and generally follow a fence on the left. On the summit of this hill where the fence turns away to the left, continue ahead for approximately 200 yards/183 m. Turn left here, and follow the path which descends steeply, finishing with another flight of steps. At the bottom of these steps, continuing across the track and through the gateway in front, walk across the golf course, initially alongside a hedge on the right. Where this hedge finishes, continue ahead to the holly bush at the right-hand end of the group of trees in the middle of the course. From this point walk slightly towards the left, heading for Beacon Hill in front, and following the intermittent line of trees. Arriving at the intruding corner of a wood, continue straight ahead along the path just inside its edge. This path now ascends gradually, and then bears round towards the left. After a few yards, bear right up the flight of steps, and follow the path which climbs steeply up the hillside.

As you ascend, a good panoramic view opens out to the right across Rubery. Frankley Beeches are prominent on top of their hill in the middle distance, and further to the right the centre of Birmingham is visible, with the University and Post Office Towers both prominent. Behind is Rednal Hill, and to its right, Cofton Hackett and the Bittell Reservoirs.

Nearing the summit, pass a trigonometrical point at the corner of a Scots pine wood. Continue straight along the edge of this, to the top of Beacon Hill.

Here there is a topographical dial on a raised plinth, from which a magnificent panoramic view of approximately 270 degrees is obtained. The Clent Hills, towards which you are now heading, are roughly in the middle of this arc. The panorama includes Cannock Chase, Dudley, Wenlock Edge, Kinver Edge, Clee Hills, Wyre Forest, Malvern Hills, and the Cotswolds.

Continue walking straight across the summit to the gateway, which is reached after walking alongside a hedge on the right. Pass through this on to the road junction, and continue ahead along the road signposted *Bromsgrove*. After approximately 550 yards/503 m, arrive at Beacon Farm on the right. Turn right here, and walk along the concrete roadway alongside the farm. The National Trust, whose Chadwich Manor Estate you are about to enter, have signposted this path, *Chadwich and Bristol Road*. Continue ahead to a gateway and stile. Cross the stile and, passing a pond on the right, follow the track round to the left. This continues and descends through a beech and larch wood. At the bottom of the wood the track turns towards the left and runs along a small valley. Passing a house on the right, go through the gateway at the end of the track and walk along the tarmac roadway. The M5 motorway can be seen some distance in front.

At the end of the roadway, turn left along the road. Proceed for a few yards and then take the first turn on the right, signposted *Rubery*, and also by the National Trust *Chadwich and Romsley*. Shortly pass under the bridge carrying the A38 trunk road. At the bottom of the slope, Chadwich Manor is on the right. The lane now starts climbing, and another National Trust signpost directs you on towards Rubery and Romsley. After approximately 600 yards/549 m, and a short distance after some cottages and houses on the left, turn left along the concrete roadway leading to Chadwich Grange Farm, and signposted by the National Trust, *Highfield and Romsley*. Cross the cattle-grid alongside the gate, and walk along the roadway.

Just before reaching the next gateway and a second cattle-grid, turn right and walk up the left-hand edge of the gently rising field. At the corner, pass through the iron kissing-gate, and turn towards the right. This is signposted *Rubery* by the National Trust. Walk up the right-hand edge of the next field, noting the excellent views which now appear behind. At the corner of this field, pass through another iron kissing-gate, and continue uphill along the right-hand edge of the next field. At its top, go through a third iron kissing-gate in the corner, and walk straight ahead up to the summit of the hill, gradually approaching the hedge on the left.

This is Highfield, from which a 300-degree view is obtained, to Birmingham in front, the Lickey Hills to the right, the Malvern Hills behind, and the Clent Hills to the left. This is also the start of the Waseley Country Park, which you now cross on your way to Windmill Hill.

From the summit, continue straight ahead to the corner of the field. Turn left here, through the gap in the hedge, and walk down the well defined path along the right-hand edge of the next field. The ground drops steeply away on the right towards Rubery. At the end of the field, pass through the gateway and continue along the right-hand edge of the following field. At the end of this, pass through the gateway and, turning right, follow the National Trust signpost towards Windmill Hill and Romsley, walking along the right-hand edge of the field. Pass through the remains of a hedge with Waseley Hill Farm to the right, and walk down the track across the next field. A few yards before reaching the gateway at the bottom, turn left and walk up the track along the bottom of the shallow cutting. This bears round to the right. At the top of it, continue along the left-hand edge of the field to the gateway at the end of the narrow neck. Pass through this, and walk along the hedged track, initially in a second shallow cutting. Frankley Beeches are prominent on their hill across to the right.

At the end of the hedged section of the track, continue along the right-hand edge of the field alongside its rather sparse hedge. Just before reaching the corner on the summit of Windmill Hill, bear slightly to the left, and pass just to the right of the intruding corner of the fence coming up from the left. Walk for a few yards beside this fence, to what was at one time the end of the field, now marked by the remains of an old hedge. From here, continue along the right-hand edge of the next field beside another sparse hedge. Cross the stile in front and, bearing slightly towards the left, walk straight down the field following to the gateway in the corner (heading towards the two adjacent radio masts on Romsley Hill beyond).

Pass through the gateway and turn left along the lane. After approximately 100 yards/91 m, bear left into Green Lane. Follow this, shortly continuing round a sharp right-hand bend. After a few yards, pass through the gateway across this lane, and turning left follow the concrete road to the bridge over the M5 motorway. Cross the bridge, and continue round to the right along the concrete road. After a few more yards, pass through a second gateway across the road and turn left along the lane, shortly arriving at a road junction. Turn right, and walk along the main A459 road to the Manchester Inn on the left.

Immediately after the inn, turn through the gateway on the left and walk ahead across the corner of the field, initially alongside a short hedge on the left. At the hedge in front (alongside a gateway) bear right, and walk up the left-hand edge of the field, alongside a wood. Go through the gateway and continue along the left-hand edge of the next field, still alongside the wood. Cross the stile, and keep on along the left-hand edge of the following field. Pass through the gateway, and continue on along the left-hand edge of the next one. Go through the gateway and, turning slightly towards the right, walk straight across the next field to the opposite corner, alongside a bungalow.

Cross the stile, and turning right, walk uphill along the lane. This is Romsley Hill. After about 150 yards/137 m, turn left along the lane signposted *Shut Mill* and *Walton Hill.* Walk the full length of this, shortly dropping steeply downhill through the woods. Turn right at the junction at the foot of the hill, and walk for a few yards along the lane to the stile on the left, opposite the entrance to Shut Mill Cottage.

Cross the stile, and climb steeply up the bank along the well defined path. From its top, the old mill pond is seen behind Shut Mill Cottage. Bear slightly towards the left, and walk straight uphill to the intruding corner where the fence and hedge, coming from the right, arrive on the skyline. From this point, continue uphill, alongside the hedge and fence on the right. Cross the fence in front and walk diagonally up the next field, heading for the gable end of the barn at Calcot Hill Farm, seen at the top. Arriving at the top edge of the field, turn right and walk along it, alongside the hedge on the left. Pass through the gateway, and walk alongside the hedge along the top edge of the hillside field which slopes steeply away down to the right. After approximately 200 yards/183 m, turn left with the hedge at the corner. Excellent views are seen across to the right.

Continue along the top of the hillside, alongside the

Standing Stones, Clent Hill

remains of a fence on the left and passing partially through an area of scrubby woodland. At the end of the field, pass through the hedge and continue along the path which now bears slightly towards the right. Shortly, and climbing gently, arrive once again alongside the remains of a fence and hedge on the left. Follow these along the top edge of this hillside field, shortly dropping down into a depression and then rising up over a ridge. On the top of this ridge turn left and, passing through the remains of a gateway, walk to the stile a few yards in front. Cross this, and walk along the top edge of the next hillside field, alongside the fence and hedge on the left. At the top of the next ridge pass through the remains of a gateway, and continue straight on along the well defined path

Near summit of Clent Hill

which shortly again runs alongside the hedge on the left. For a few yards along this section, the path runs between the remains of old hedges. Continue through the gateway at the end of this stretch, and walk along the left-hand edge of the next field. Cross the stile, and following the fence on the left, pass Walton Hill Farm.

Cross the stile and, turning left, walk for a few yards along the farm driveway, almost to the gateway. Bear to the right here along the adjoining track for a few more yards, and then turning right into another track, follow this through the gorse to the top of the hill. Near the summit, join a track running up diagonally from the left, and continue to the trigonometrical point on the top of Walton Hill. The 360-

North West from Clent Hill

degree panoramic view obtained from here, at a height of 1,035 ft/315 m, includes the Black Country directly in front. Continue straight on along the top of the hill, and at the end of the ridge, drop steeply down to the road.

Turning left, walk along the road and after about a $\frac{1}{4}$-mile/400 m turn right at the junction signposted *Hasbury* and *Halesowen*. Walk for a short distance to Hagley Wood Lane on the left, signposted *Hayley Green*. Turn up this lane, and follow it for about 300 yards/274 m to the top of the hill. Turn left here into the woodland, and climb the steep track alongside the fence on the left, just inside the edge of the woods. After leaving the trees, follow the track along the top of the ridge and shortly arrive at a trigonometrical point, four

Folly at Adams Hill

standing stones, and slightly to the left a topographical dial on a plinth. This indicates the magnificent, almost 360-degree view to be seen from here on the top of Clent Hill. The view includes the Cotswolds, Cleeve Hill, Worcester, the Malverns, the Black Mountains, the Clee Hills, the Long Mynd, the Wrekin, Kinver Edge, and Cannock Chase.

Return to the trig point, and continue along the gently descending track following the summit ridge. Arriving alongside a small clump of Scots pines on the left, leave the main track which bears off towards the left, and continuing straight ahead, drop down to the right of the summit ridge, passing close to an area of scrubby oak woodland on the right. The path shortly becomes more well defined, where it drops steeply downhill to Adams Hill village in the hollow. Here are the Hill Tavern, a restaurant, and a refreshment bar. The track finishes with a short stretch between a wall and a fence. At its end, turn right and walk down the road to the Fountain Inn at the junction.

A most interesting double-towered castle-like folly can be seen inside the grounds of Clent Grove, a children's home, the entrance to which is just round to the right.

STOURBRIDGE
KIDDERMINSTER
Kinver
Rockmount
Whittington
Dunsley
The Lodge
Bunkers Hill
Norton
Old Swinford
STOURBRIDGE JN
A 4036
Hodge Hill
Wollescote
The Quarry
Pedmore
Hall
Wychbury Hill
WYCHBURY
A 456
Elm Lo.
202m
Hagley
The Birches
Hagley Park
Hall
Clent Grove
Catchems End
A 451
Cookley
Lower Hagley
West Hagley
Ismere Ho.
Churchill
A 449
R. Stour
Lea Castle
Stakenbridge
Field Ho.
Adams Hill
Clent Hills
Clent
Holy Cross
Walton Ho.
Moor Hall
The Grange
Belbroughton Lo.
Waterley Co.
Heathfield
Sionhill Ho.
Broadwaters
Wood Ho.
Blakedown
STA
B 4188
Park Hall
Hurcott
A 456
Yieldingtree
Brookfield
Yewtree Ho.
Bell Hall
Hartle
Belbroughton
Bradford Ho.
Sion Ho.
A 491
Bell End
Hall
Iron Ho.
Kinver Edge
Drakelow

5 **Adams Hill – Holy Cross – Broome – Churchill – Caunsall – Kinver Edge**

Distance: 9¾ miles/15.7 km

Leave Adams Hill by Violet Lane opposite the Fountain Inn. Walk the length of this, and passing under the main A491 road at the roundabout, bear left along the road signposted *Bromsgrove*. After approximately a ¼-mile/400 m, and having passed a barn on the right, turn right beside a cottage and follow the concrete footpath, signposted *Broome*. At the end of the cottage garden, pass through the wooden gate and, after a few more yards, a second gate. Go through this, and walking between a wall and bushes, cross the stile and follow the left-hand edge of the field. A few yards before reaching the end of this, go through the gateway on the left, and continue straight on along the right-hand edge of the next field. Pass through the gateway and walk along the edge of the following field. Continue through the hedge at the end of this, and follow the right-hand edge of the next field. At the corner, drop steeply down on to the lane.

Turn right and walk down the lane for about 150 yards/137 m, and then turn through the gateway on the left, following the signpost to Broome. Walk along the right-hand edge of the field. Cross the stile, and walk along the right-hand edge of the following field. Cross the stile, and continue along the right-hand edge of the next field, now along a well defined track. At the end of this field, continue along the track which now runs between hedges. After a sharp left-hand bend, the track (now tarmac) arrives at a junction with a lane on the right. Turn right, and walk along this, shortly passing a house on the left called The Old Well.

Continue through Broome village, passing the church of St Peter (dating from the eighteenth century but containing a small Norman font) and bear left at the junction, following the signpost towards Churchill. After approximately a ¼-mile/400 m, turn left along the main A450 road. Follow this for about 300 yards/274 m, to the end of the first field on the right

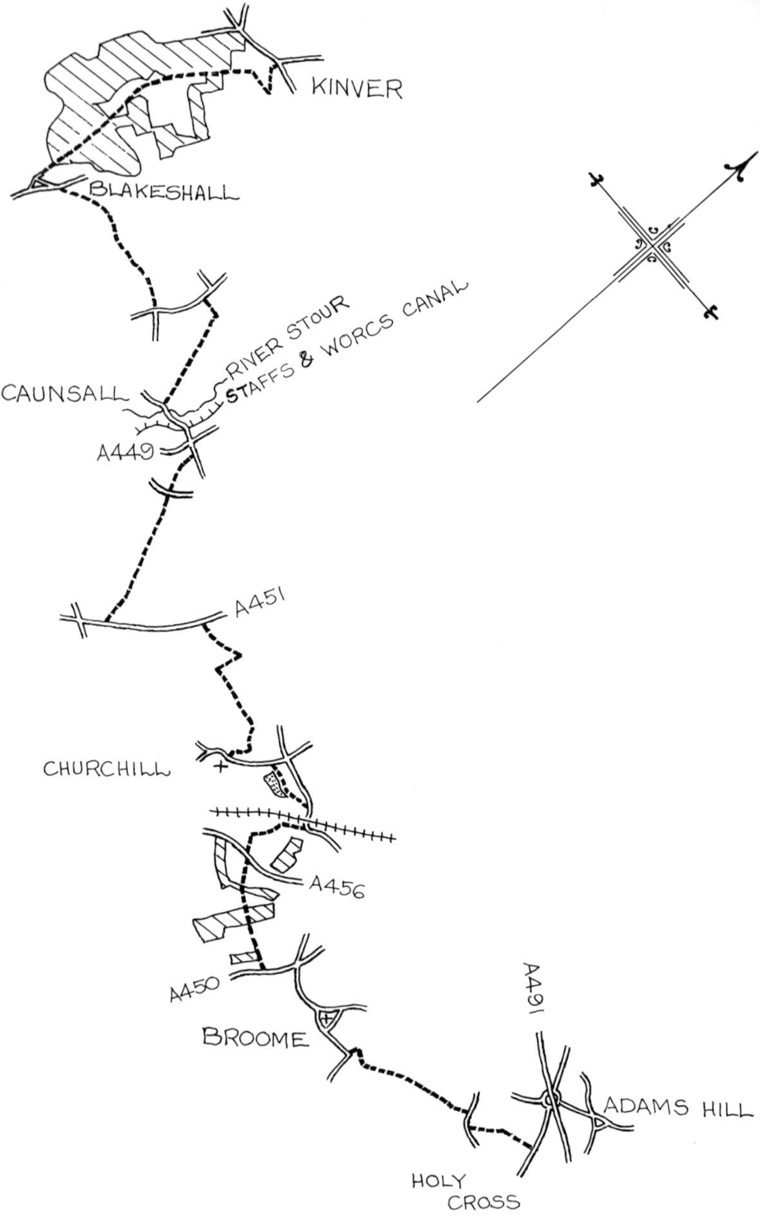
KINVER
BLAKESHALL
RIVER STOUR
STAFFS & WORCS CANAL
CAUNSALL
A449
A451
CHURCHILL
A456
A450
BROOME
A491
ADAMS HILL
HOLY
CROSS

St Peter's, Broome

after passing Broome Lodge Farm. At this point, turn through the gateway on the right, following the signpost towards Harborough Hill.

Walk along the right-hand edge of the field, and at the end of this, pass through the gateway and continue along the right-hand edge of the one following. At the end of this field, continue along the track into the wood, passing an old industrial building on the left. A short way past this, continue over the cross-track, and walk downhill through the trees. Cross the stile at the bottom of the wood, and walk straight across the field in front to a point just to the right of the house at the far side. Pass through the gateway here, and cross the embankment between the two lakes. Go through the gateway and, bearing towards the left, walk straight across the field. Once the brow of this field is reached, a stile can be seen in the hedge in front.

Cross the stile and, turning left, walk for a few yards along the main A456 road. Then, turning right, cross the fence into the corner of the field, following the signpost towards Churchill. Walk along the right-hand edge of this field, and at the corner turn through the gateway on the right. Proceed along the left-hand edge of the next field. The wooded Harborough Hill is just across to the right. At the end of the field, pass through the gateway in front and walk along the hedged and fenced path. After some distance this drops downhill, and continues as a track to the road alongside the railway bridge.

Turn left under the bridge, and follow the road between

Footpath to Churchill

two lakes and then round to the left. Immediately after this left-hand bend, bear left through the gateway following the *Churchill* signpost. Walk along the left-hand edge of the field. At the end of this, pass through the unusual iron slot stile, and cross the next field to the stile just to the right of the gateway in front. Cross this stile, and walk beside the lake on the left. Near the end of this, pass through a second iron slot stile, and continue to the iron kissing-gate at the end of the lake. Pass through this and proceed along the path in front. Almost immediately join a track coming from the left, and follow this to the lane.

Turn left, and walk along the lane for approximately a $\frac{1}{4}$-

Slot Stile, near Churchill

mile/400 m to St James' church, Churchill, built in 1868. Turn right opposite here, and walk up the track signposted *Rocky Lane*, initially passing an old ivy-covered barn on the left, and then an old timber-clad barn on the right. At the end of this track, pass through the gateway into the field, and turning left walk uphill along its left-hand edge. Cross the fence in front, and turning right walk straight up to the summit of the hill, keeping fairly near to the fence. A magnificent 360-degree panoramic view is obtained from the top. Turn left in the corner here, and walk along the top edge of the field, alongside the fence on the right. At the next corner continue straight ahead through the remains of a gateway, and after a few yards cross the stile on the right, alongside the next gateway. Turn left, and walk for a few more yards, now with the fence on the left, and enter the end of a hedged track. Walk down the length of this, passing a track on the left, and at the end turn right along the cross-track. After about 200 yards/183 m, turn left through the gateway into the corner of the field. Walk along the right-hand edge of this, and passing through the gateway, continue along the left-hand edge of the next field. Go through the gateway on to the main A451 road. Just along to the right is the Wagon and Horses Inn.

Turn left and walk along the main road for approximately a ½-mile/800 m past the two driveways to Ismere House, to a track on the right signposted *Public Footpath–Caunsall.* Turn right, and follow this track along the right-hand edge of the field. Go through the gateway and continue along the right-hand edge of the following field. Arriving alongside the large pond on the right, the track continues to the right of the hedge in front, and bears right up to Whitehouse Farm. However, your path continues straight ahead up the shallow depression, and passes to the left of the farmhouse. At the top of this depression, cross the stile, and turning towards the left walk straight across the field, heading for a point just to the left of the church which is seen on the skyline. Cross the stile in the hedge in front, and continue straight across the next field, still on the same heading. Good views are now seen ahead to the higher ground around Kinver Edge. Go through the gateway in front at the corner of the field, and walk straight across the following field, heading for the Dutch barn at the far side. Pass to the right of this, and immediately bearing left arrive at the gateway leading on to the lane.

Pass through the gateway, and turning right, walk along the lane. After a few yards, turn through the first gateway on the left, signposted *Caunsall.* Walk straight ahead across the corner of the field and, arriving at the hedge on the left, continue beside this to the gateway in the corner. Pass through this, and turning left walk down the lane.

Cross straight over the main A449 road, and continue along the lane opposite, signposted *Caunsall* $\frac{1}{2}$ *mile* (800 m). After a few yards, cross the Staffordshire and Worcestershire Canal, and shortly the River Stour. Just over the bridge, and immediately after the tarmac driveway to a farm, turn right

River Stour, Caunsall

through the hedge into the field corner (this may present some difficulty, and an alternative is to follow the driveway, passing between the house and farm buildings, then go through the gateway, and turning left across the end of the rickyard, go through the next gateway into the same field, then turn right). Walk along the right-hand edge of this very large field, following the fairly well defined track. Pass through the gateway, and continue along the track which now runs alongside a wire fence on the left-hand edge of the following field. At the end of this, turn left across the fence and walk along the right-hand end of the next field to the gateway.

Go through the gateway, and turning left walk along the lane for approximately a $\frac{1}{4}$-mile/400 m. Turn through the gateway on the right, opposite a lane, and walk along a short track. At the end of this, pass through a second gateway, and continue straight ahead, and walk between the double line of trees in front. Follow these along the bottom of a shallow valley. Arriving alongside a cottage on the right called The Sladd, continue through the gateway in front, to the left of the barn, and walk along the hedged track. At the end of this section, pass through the hedge and walk along the left-hand edge of the field in front. Pass through the hedge at the end of this, and continue straight on, once again along a hedged track. After about 600 yards/549 m, pass straight over a cross-track, and follow the track along the right-hand edge of a field, alongside gorse bushes.

At the end of the track, turn left along the lane. After a few yards, and now in Blakeshall, bear right along the well defined track, which shortly turns sharp right on joining another track coming from the left. Follow this hedged track, and at the point where it bears left, continue straight ahead through the split fence in front. Walk ahead for several yards, avoiding the track which bears off to the right, and shortly pass through a second split fence, now entering the pine woodland of Kinver Edge. Walk straight ahead along the path through the trees, and after a short distance pass through a double split fence at a cross-track, and continue straight on along the path.

Crossing the next track, continue straight on, now passing more mature woodland carpeted with heather and fern. The path is now gently climbing over sandy ground. Continue ahead at the next cross-track, once again passing through split fences. Here you leave Worcestershire, and enter Staffordshire.

Still climbing, walk straight ahead alongside a wire fence on the right. Near the summit of the climb and having passed a wood on the right, arrive at the remains of an iron kissing-gate. Continue across the track in front, and bearing slightly to the left, enter the National Trust land of Kinver Edge. Walk along the path, which after about 100 yards/91 m joins the main path along the Edge. Turn right and walk along this.

Rock dwelling, Holy Austin Rock, Kinver

The ground drops very steeply away to the left, revealing excellent views across to Enville Hall and its surrounding parkland. Note the good views behind you, over Kidderminster and beyond, and across to the right towards the Clent Hills.

Pass a trigonometrical point at the top of the Edge, and continuing over the site of an Iron Age fort, walk to the end of the ridge. From here you look out over Kinver village and across the Black Country. Directly below you in front is Holy Austin Rock. Follow the path, which now bears round to the right and starts descending, at first gradually, and then more steeply. Arriving at the open grassy area at the bottom of this steep section, bear completely round to the left and follow the path down below the Edge.

The path is now leading directly towards Holy Austin Rock, but turns down to the right a short distance before reaching it. However, a detour to look at the rock is essential, because of its great and unique interest. It is hollowed out into dwellings with rooms, passages, and caves on varying levels. These possibly date back to Celtic times, and were occupied as recently as the 1940s. At its northern end the sandstone is weathered into gently rounded forms, clearly showing the strata.

Returning to the path, continue down it to the road. You are now in the outskirts of Kinver, the centre of which is some way to the right. Turn left, and walk along the road for a short distance, to the junction below Holy Austin Rock.

Bridgnorth
The Hermitage
Barnsley
Woundale
Chyknell
Claverley
Aston
Draycott
Feiashall
Whittimere
Heathton
Sandford
Farmcote Hall
Up. Farmcote
Beobridge
Broughton
Halfpenny Green
Halfpenny Green
Gospelash
Smestow
Swindon
Bobbington
Leaton Hall
Highgate Common
Lower Beobridge
Morfe Valley
Gatacre
Gatacre Park
Bobbington Hall
Stanmore Hall
Danesford
Quatford Cas.
Firgrove
Quatford
BURT CAS
A 458
A 442
Oldbury
Westwood
The Hill
Eardington
Mose
Mor Brook
Eudon Burnell
Uplands
Woodlands
Crowford
Dudmaston Hall
Wooton
Quatt
Kingsnordley
Six Ashes
Tuckhill Hall
Dudhill
Four Ashes
Philley Brook
Morfe Ha. Fm
Hoo Fm
Blundies
Gilbert's Cross
Enville
Elm Ho.
Enville Hall
The Lyons
Glazeley
Borle Brook
Chelmarsh Resr.
Deuxhill
Sch.
Sutton
Wadeley
Severn Valley Rly
Hampton
Coton Hall
Little Woodlands
Moor Lo.
Turleygreen
Bindsgreen
Billetts
Bowhills Dingle
Bowhills
Sheepwalks
Compton
204m
Billingsley
B 4363
Plym Hall
Brock Hall
Hawkswood
Hazelwell
Woodhill
Hadleys
Alveley
Highley
Ford
Chorley
Netherton
Pool Hall
Ferry
Hartsgreen
Romsley
Iron Ho.
Greyfields
Kinver
Rockmount
Dunsley
Potter's Cross
Gallowstree Elm
Heathlands
Stourton Hall
Prestwood
Gothersley
Hinksford
B 4176
71m
63m
118

6 **Kinver – The Sheepwalks – Birdsgreen – Hampton Loade – Chelmarsh – Bridgnorth**

Distance: 15 miles/24·1 km

From the road junction near Holy Austin Rock at Kinver, walk down the road opposite. After about 250 yards/229 m, turn into the first road on the left. Follow this for just over 100 yards/91 m into a housing estate, and then, where it bears right, continue straight ahead along the tarmac footpath between the houses. Follow this path to the end of the back gardens, and turn right with it for a few more yards. At the end of the path, turn left across the stile into the field. Walk straight ahead across this, to the stile at the far side near the two electricity poles. Cross this stile, and continue along the track in front for a few yards; and then when it bears to the left, walk straight ahead along the fairly well defined footpath through rather scrubby woodland, and alongside a fence and hedge on the right. Cross the very dilapidated remains of an iron kissing-gate, and walk along the hedged and fenced path. Near its end, the path descends gently through a small coppice to its finish between two stone posts opposite a lane junction.

Turn right, and walk up the lane for about 150 yards/137 m to where it bends sharply right, and then continue ahead into the track, which gradually descends towards the left in a shallow cutting. Follow this track to its end, and crossing the stile alongside the gate, turn left along the lane.

After approximately 700 yards/640 m, arrive at a lane junction immediately after Compton House on the left. Take the right-hand fork, signposted *No Mans Green* and *Coxgreen*, and climb quite steeply up the lane, shortly passing a farm in a sharp right-hand bend. After a few more yards the lane bends round sharply to the left. Just under 100 yards/91 m from this bend, arrive at a gateway on the right, signposted *Coxgreen*. Go through this gateway and turn left, immediately crossing the stile over the fence in front.

The very large expanse of parkland which you are about to enter is called The Sheepwalks, and the landowner has gone

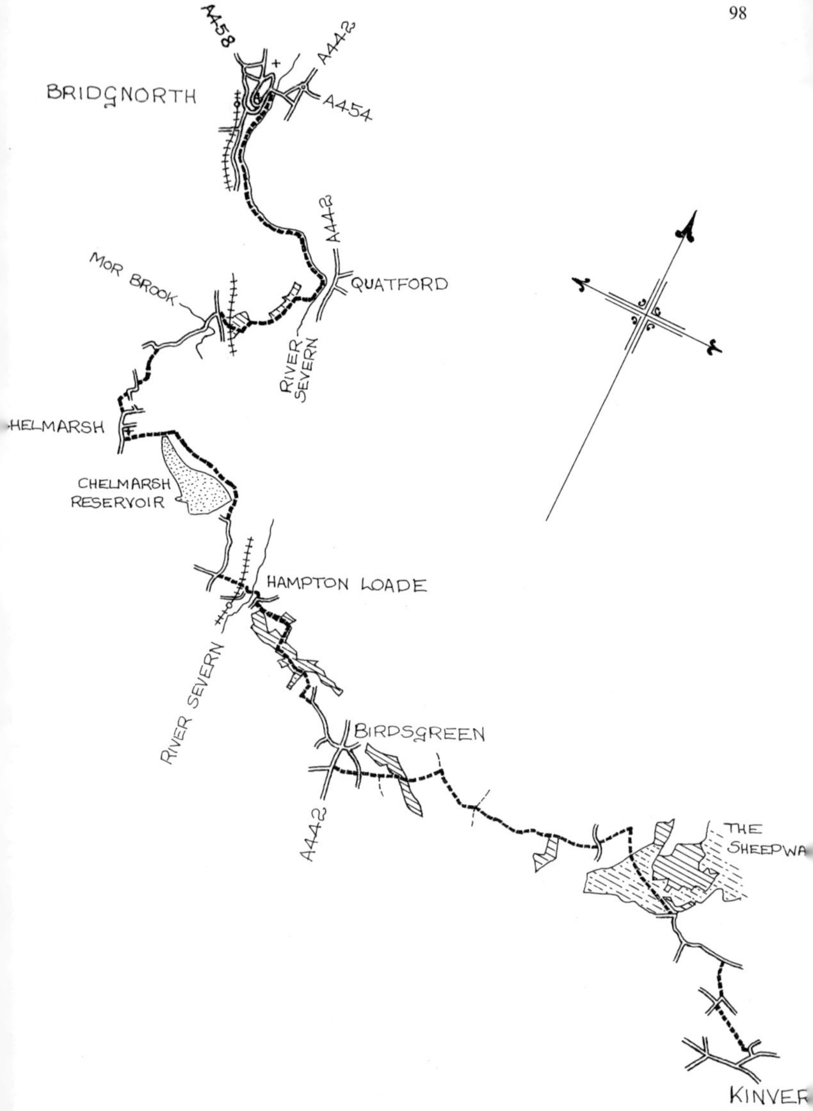
A458
A442
BRIDGNORTH
A454
A442
MOR BROOK
QUATFORD
RIVER SEVERN
HELMARSH
CHELMARSH RESERVOIR
HAMPTON LOADE
RIVER SEVERN
BIRDSGREEN
A442
THE SHEEPWA
KINVER

to a deal of trouble in waymarking the footpaths across his land, as is indicated by the notice adjoining the stile, which reads *Footpath marked by posts . . .*

From the stile, the path bears slightly towards the right and runs uphill towards the brow of the field, where the first post is clearly seen. All the posts are similar, about 6 ft/1·8 m tall, 5 ins/127 mm square, and each carrying a wooden plaque bearing the letters FP, and a double arrow. Excellent views are seen from this very high area, including the Clent Hills, Kinver Edge, and the Malvern Hills. After climbing fairly steeply to the first post, the path continues less steeply, and roughly parallel to the woodland on the right, to the second post which is just after the end of this woodland. The path now bears slightly towards the right, and runs straight to what appears to be the highest part of the area, passing to the right of the group of trees and following the line of posts across the summit of the parkland. Good views are now seen down the valley to the right, towards the Black Country. The path, continuing over the summit, passes to the left of another group of trees. Some distance across to the left is seen the ruin of a round, battlemented folly. Alongside this second group of trees, the path starts descending towards a further post, which is seen on a slight ridge some way in front. From this post, the path drops steeply downhill to the final post, just to the left of the large New Pool which is seen at the bottom of the slope.

Just past the final post, cross the stile, and bearing slightly right walk along the right-hand edge of the field, initially passing alongside the pool. FP plaques are still in evidence, marking the paths in this area, but are now fixed to trees and fences. After gradually climbing, cross the stile at the top of the field, and continue along the right-hand edge of the next one. At the end of this, immediately before the pond just over the fence in front, turn left, and continue along this next edge of the field alongside the fence on the right. Go through the gateway, and continue along the right-hand edge of the following field. Arriving alongside the group of three trees in the field, bear towards the left, and walk across the corner of the field to the gateway in front, with the farm buildings beyond.

Go through the gateway, and turning left walk along the lane for a few yards, and then turn right along the track leading between the farm buildings of The Hollies. In crossing the farmyard and passing the farm buildings, go through four gateways in fairly close succession, and continue along the hedged track in front. After about 300 yards/274 m the track turns sharp right, passing over the county boundary into Shropshire; and after a few more yards, turning sharp left, continues gently downhill. Arriving at the wood, turn right and, proceeding for a few yards, turn left and walk along the left-hand edge of the field alongside the wood. Pass through the gateway, and joining a very good track continue ahead along this, soon passing through another gateway. Follow this hedged and fenced track, and shortly turn sharp right with it. After a few more yards, turn left through the gateway and walk alongside a Dutch barn. Pass through another gateway immediately after this, and walk ahead along the narrow field to the gateway at the far end, noting the good views in front. Go through this gateway, and walk along the left-hand edge of the next field. Arriving alongside a small pond on the left, continue straight ahead across the neck of the field to rejoin the left-hand edge near a gate. Continue along this edge, and pass through the gateway at the end of the field. Bearing slightly towards the right, walk diagonally across the corner of the next field and join its right-hand edge just after the pond. Continue along this edge, and cross the fence in front at the corner. Walk ahead along the rather overgrown hedged path. Initially the hedges here are fairly wide apart, but soon narrow to normal track width. Near the end of this path, cross a wire fence and carry on to a cross-track.

Continue over the cross-track into a wooded area, and after a few yards cross the stream and walk up the just-discernible track. This runs for a short distance, just inside the right-hand edge of the wooded head of Perryhouse Dingle, while the stream drops down to the left over a waterfall, between steep banks carpeted with bluebells and wild garlic. Leaving the wooded area, the track, fairly overgrown in parts, climbs gently between hedges. Continuing uphill, the latter part of the track is clear, and good views are seen across to the left. At the top of the climb, go through the gateway and continue along the left-hand edge of the fairly small field. Just before reaching the gateway in front leading to Astley Farm, turn through the gateway on the left and walk along the right-hand end of the small paddock. Cross the fence in the corner, and walk straight across the field in front, heading for a point to the left of the ruined barn, seen just below the skyline at the top of the field immediately beyond the wooded bottom of the valley. Cross the hedge and ditch at the far side of the field, approximately 100 yards/91 m to the left of the two solitary trees in the hedge, and continue across the next field, now heading almost directly towards our landmark barn.

This brings you to the tree at the intruding field corner coming from the right, some way before the bottom of the field. Cross the fence here into the corner of the next field, and walking diagonally towards the right, drop fairly steeply downhill to a point at the bottom of this field about 100 yards/91 m to the right of the left-hand corner. Cross the fence here, and still following the line of our diagonal, drop steeply down into the wooded Bowhills Dingle. There is no visible path here, and care is needed in avoiding branches and undergrowth. Cross the stream at the bottom; there is no bridge, but several places may be found where crossing is possible. Still following the same diagonal, climb up the opposite side, and cross the fence at the top into the field, covered in this area with a scattering of trees. Turn right, and walk along the edge of this field alongside the boundary of the dingle. Shortly bear left with the field edge and, climbing up hill, arrive at the top corner of the field. Cross the fence in front, and walk up the right-hand edge of the next field (your landmark barn is across to the left at the top of this). Go through the gateway, and bearing right walk along the hedged track. Birdsgreen is down to the right, and Alveley village with its church is prominent in front.

At the end of the track, cross straight over the lane and, climbing the low bank, cross the fence and walk along the left-hand edge of the field. Cross the fence, and continue straight on along the left-hand edge of the grassed area to the main A442 road. The Royal Oak Inn is just along to the left.

Turn right, and walk along the main road for about 300 yards/274 m to the crossroads at Birdsgreen, passing the Squirrel Inn on the left. Turn left here, and walk along the lane signposted *Turley Green.* After about 250 yards/229 m, where this bends left to Alveley, continue straight ahead along the minor lane in front. Follow this lane to its end (approximately 700 yards/640 m), at the point where it turns

Into Lakehouse Dingle

sharp right and continues as the private driveway to Lake House. From this right-hand bend, continue straight on along the hedged track in front to a point opposite the end of the first field on the left, and just before the track becomes rather overgrown. Turn right here through the gap in the hedge, and walk straight ahead across the field. Cross the wooden fence in the hedge in front, and bearing slightly towards the left, walk across the corner of the next field to the slightly intruding corner that is clearly seen at the edge of the wooded dingle on the left. Just before reaching the dingle, walk to the left of the short line of trees in the field. Cross the wooden fence in front, and follow the obvious path down into the wooded Lakehouse Dingle.

Waterfall, Lakehouse Dingle

Arriving alongside the stream at the bottom of the dingle, a larger stream is seen immediately in front, running out of Gortens Dingle on the right. Avoid the stone slab bridge in front over this second stream, and turning left cross the smaller stream at its confluence with the larger one, and walk along the left-hand bank of the larger stream. The dingle is carpeted with many varieties of wild flowers, including primroses, violets, wood anemones, lesser celandines, marsh marigolds, and daffodils. Shortly pass a stepped waterfall. The fairly well defined path keeps near to the stream along the bottom of the dingle, which is now becoming shallower and less steep-sided. After a while the stream opens out into a pleasant pool surrounded by woodland. Pass through the gap in the fence alongside the dam at the end of the pool, and turn right down the path to the bridge at the foot of the spillway. Cross this bridge, and passing through the gate continue up the well defined path through the woodland. At the top of this, pass through the gate and turn left.

Walk along the good track, which immediately bears right and continues gently uphill between trees. Turn left through the gateway at the top of the first field, and walk along its right-hand edge alongside a wood. Continue along this edge of the field to where it turns sharply away to the right. From this point continue straight ahead across the remainder of the field, heading for the prominent white house which is clearly seen in front across the valley of the River Severn. Your path passes a few yards to the right of the electricity pylon in the field. At the wooded edge of the field turn right, and walk down this. Still descending, shortly walk alongside a hedge on the left. Near the foot of the slope, and just before reaching the house behind this hedge, turn left across the fence. Walk along the left-hand edge of the garden of this house (a café), to the gate leading on to the lane in front, in the village of Hampton Loade. A short way to the left is the Lion Inn.

Turn right along the lane for a few yards, and at the sharp right-hand bend continue ahead into the car park alongside the River Severn, to the landing stage for the ferry across the river. A bell-push is located on a telegraph pole here, to summon the ferry operator. Cross the river by this ferry, for which a toll is payable and which operates at most times, except when the river is in flood.

From the opposite landing stage, walk diagonally to the right across the open stretch of land to its top corner. Pass through the gap here and arrive in front of the Unicorn Inn. Continue up the slope alongside the inn fence and, passing through the gateway at the top, cross the Severn Valley Railway. A regular service of steam-hauled trains runs along this line, and there is a station a short distance to the left which is reached by following the roadway opposite the Unicorn Inn.

Chain ferry across River Severn

Climb the bank and, passing through the gateway at the top, walk up the right-hand edge of the very small field. Cross the stile, and walk straight across the large field in front, heading for a point at the far side, just to the right of the bungalow (itself some yards to the right of the large white house that was your earlier landmark). Pass to the right of the bungalow, and continue alongside a hedge to the stile at the corner in front.

Cross the stile, and turn right along the lane. A notice indicates that this is the road to Millfields. After about 600 yards/549 m the dam of Chelmarsh Reservoir is prominent in front. The lane now descends, and crosses a cattle-grid. Where it bends sharply to the left, continue on downhill alongside the fence on the right, signposted *Public Footpath*. Cross the

Severn Valley Railway

brook at the bottom of the slope, and climb up the hedged and fenced track in front. Near the top of this, pass the Chelmarsh Sailing Club at the end of the reservoir. Pass through the gateway in front at the top of the hill, and immediately turn through the gateway on the left into the field. The reservoir now spreads its length below you. Walk diagonally across the field to a point approximately 100 yards/91 m to the right of its far left-hand corner. This is not visible for several yards, and the initial heading is towards the head of the first indent along the shore of the reservoir. Cross the fence in front, and bearing slightly towards the left walk straight across the next field, heading for a point slightly to the right of the church tower on the skyline in front.

Once the low brow of this field is crossed, a gate is seen in the hedge in front. Pass through this, and walk along the right-hand edge of the next field. To turn around is rewarding, for there are excellent views back across the reservoir towards the clubhouse and beyond. Pass through the gateway, and walk along a short track beside a pond on the left. Continue on along the right-hand edge of the field to the gateway between the farm buildings and the Dutch barn. Pass through this gateway and walk for a few yards along the farm track, to its end at a cross-track. Turn left here, and follow the track downhill towards the head of the reservoir. At the bottom of the slope pass through the gateway, and then shortly through a second, and continue along the fenced track across the head of the reservoir.

Pass through another gateway at the end of this section, and walk up the fairly steep-hedged track in front. Some way up the slope, pass through a gateway and continue up the track, which now runs in a shallow-hedged cutting. Near the top of this, pass some farm buildings on the right with Chelmarsh church just beyond. Go through the gateway at the top of the track, and turn right along the lane. The Bulls Head Inn is just along to the left.

Follow the lane, passing St Peter's church, Chelmarsh, and a lane on the right. The eighteenth-century tower of the church contains a rare clock, possibly the oldest in the county.

Bear left at the telephone kiosk where the lane swings round to the right and descends into the valley, and walk along the track in front of Manor Farm. A few yards after passing the large house on the right of this track, turn through the second of the two almost adjacent gates on the right, and walk along the right-hand edge of the field at the bottom of a shallow cutting. Cross the stile, immediately passing a cottage on the left, and turn left along the lane. Follow this round a right-hand bend, to the gateway in front at the sharp left-hand bend. Pass through this gateway and, turning towards the left, walk diagonally down the field, heading for the large house which can be seen some way in front. The Severn valley extends in front towards Bridgnorth. Near a gateway in the bottom edge of the field, turn left and walk along this edge. At the end of the field, and a few yards before reaching the Dutch barn, cross the fence on the right into the adjacent field. Walk diagonally to the left down this, heading for the hedge intersection between the two fields beyond (a tree and an electricity pole mark this point). Cross the fence into the corner of the left-hand of the two fields, and walk diagonally to the left up this, to the gateway at the left-hand end of the skyline. Pass through this gateway, and bearing right walk along the lane.

Pass Astbury Hall on the right after about 350 yards/320 m, and continue down the lane into the valley of the Mor Brook. Cross the bridge at the bottom, noting the high waterfall on the left, and continue up to the road junction at the top of the climb. Cross the lane in front, and go through the gateway opposite into the corner of the field. Ignore the *Trespassers Will Be Prosecuted* sign, as in law this cannot apply to a public right of way providing one keeps to the defined route. Turn towards the right and walk diagonally down the field to the bottom edge, at the point adjacent to the middle of the three telegraph poles on the embankment of the Severn Valley Railway. Arriving at this point, turn towards the right along the edge of the field. Shortly, and just before the field edge starts rising steeply, turn left and cross the fenced remains of a gate into the accommodation tunnel running beneath the railway.

At the far end of the tunnel, turn towards the right (ignoring the sign *Private Property, please keep out* as this too, does not apply to the right of way), and follow the just discernible path running diagonally away from the railway through the stretch of woodland, keeping just to the right of the foot of the slope. Just before reaching the fence in front along the edge of the woodland, turn left and walk along the fairly well defined path inside the wood's edge. This area is carpeted with bluebells in season. Cross the fence in front alongside the end of the field on the right and, leaving the woodland, walk straight over the cross-track, and cross the fence in front alongside the tree. Walk across the large field, initially heading slightly towards the right, and dropping gradually into the shallow valley running down it.

Arriving just below the group of oaks on the bank to the left, continue straight on along the left-hand side of the valley bottom, keeping parallel to the fence and hedge across to the right, and heading for the right-hand corner of the belt of woodland running away in front at the end of the field. Cross the wooden fence into the right-hand corner of this woodland, and walk ahead along the path just inside its right-hand edge. Arriving alongside the end of the first field, cross the fence on the right into the corner of the second field, and continue along the left-hand edge of this, outside the woodland. Quatford village is seen across the valley in front. Turn right in the corner of the field, and continue along its end, alongside the hedge on the left. At the next corner, turn through the gateway on the left. Turning towards the right, walk diagonally across the corner of the next field, to the bank of the River Severn (the heading is towards the right-hand end of the rock face across the river).

Turn left and walk alongside the river. Cross the fence at the end of the field, and continue along the river bank, passing Quatford village across to the right. Cross the next fence and continue ahead, noting Quatford Castle and Quatford House, also to the right. Continue straight on at the end of this field, and similarly at the end of the next, along the path which now continues as a track below a rocky bank beside the river. At the end of this track, the path continues on along the river bank, once again with a field on the left. Bridgnorth's High Town and its two churches are now seen some way in front. Cross the stile at the end of the field, and continue, now with a fence on the left and then shortly a hedge. After crossing a stream, the path continues with a road just above it to the left. Crossing another fence in front, the path now runs along the edge of a riverside meadow, which has the embankment of the Severn Valley Railway above the road along its left-hand side. The remains of the walls of Bridgnorth Castle, and the tower of St Mary's church, are now prominent in front on top of the High Town Rock.

Cross a small brook and a fence at the end of the meadow, and follow the path along the river bank, noting over to the left the railway station, and beyond it the peculiarly named Panpudding Hill. Cross the stile in front, and continue along the path, which once again has a fence and hedge along its left-hand side. High Town is now above you, and the bridge joining the High and Low Towns is directly in front. The path shortly runs along the backs of gardens and other properties, and finishes in a small ornamental garden just before the bridge. Your route continues over the bridge, but a detour to see the town of Bridgnorth is well worth while.

Bridgnorth perambulation

Opposite the end of the bridge is the entrance to the lower station of the cliff railway, which can be used (for a small charge) to avoid the steep climb up to the main town. For those who prefer to walk up, turn up the steep narrow street on the right. This is Cartway, and some way up on its right are the bricked-up entrances to old cave-dwellings which were

The leaning keep, Bridgnorth Castle

occupied until 1856. Near the top, turn left into Castle Terrace which leads to Castle Walk and the upper station of the cliff railway. This is an excellent viewpoint from which to look out over the river and the Low Town.

Arriving alongside the church of St Mary Magdalene, turn right and follow the path to the front of it. This church, dated 1792, is the work of the great engineer Thomas Telford, and is situated at the end of a specially arranged street vista.

Continue along the path at the side of the churchyard, and then turning left walk to the Castle ruins and into the Castle grounds. Very little now remains of this twelfth-century Norman building, but it is remarkable for the keep which is leaning precariously at an angle of approximately 17 degrees from the vertical. The town war memorial, in the form of a statue of a soldier of the First World War, is of note because it is the work of Captain Adrian Jones, who is famous for the Quadriga at Hyde Park Corner.

Leaving the Castle grounds, which command excellent views from the end of the Castle rock, pass to the opposite side of the ruins and out through the main gates. Turning left and crossing the road, take the footpath almost opposite, leading steeply down to the left. At the bottom, turn right along the main road, and then shortly turn left up into the yard of the station and headquarters of the Severn Valley Railway Company. This preservation organization has taken over the line from Bridgnorth to Bewdley and runs it on a commercial basis as a working steam museum. Many old and interesting steam locomotives, together with their rolling-stock, can be seen in and around the station area, and a trip along the line is a memorable event.

Returning to the road, turn left and then right almost opposite, and walk to the top of the street. Turn right here to the town centre. At the High Street turn left, and walk along this main shopping street, passing the town hall with its timbered upper storey supported on open stone arches above the roadway beneath, and dating from 1652. The High Street contains several buildings of the eighteenth and nineteenth centuries, and across its end stands the Northgate, originally built in 1740 and restored in 1910.

Just before reaching the Northgate, turn right up Church Street, and right again at the top. St Leonard's church, standing in its open grassed area surrounded by a miscellany of almshouses, cottages, and other eighteenth-century buildings (much like a cathedral close), is mainly Victorian, dated 1860–1862. Palmers Hospital, on the right, has a half-timbered upper floor, and is built around three sides of a courtyard.

Shortly, turn right down St Leonards Steps, and passing through the arch at the bottom, rejoin Cartway. Bishop Percy's House on the left was built in 1580, and contains some excellent black and white work. Continue down Cartway, to the river bridge at the bottom.

Northgate, Bridgnorth

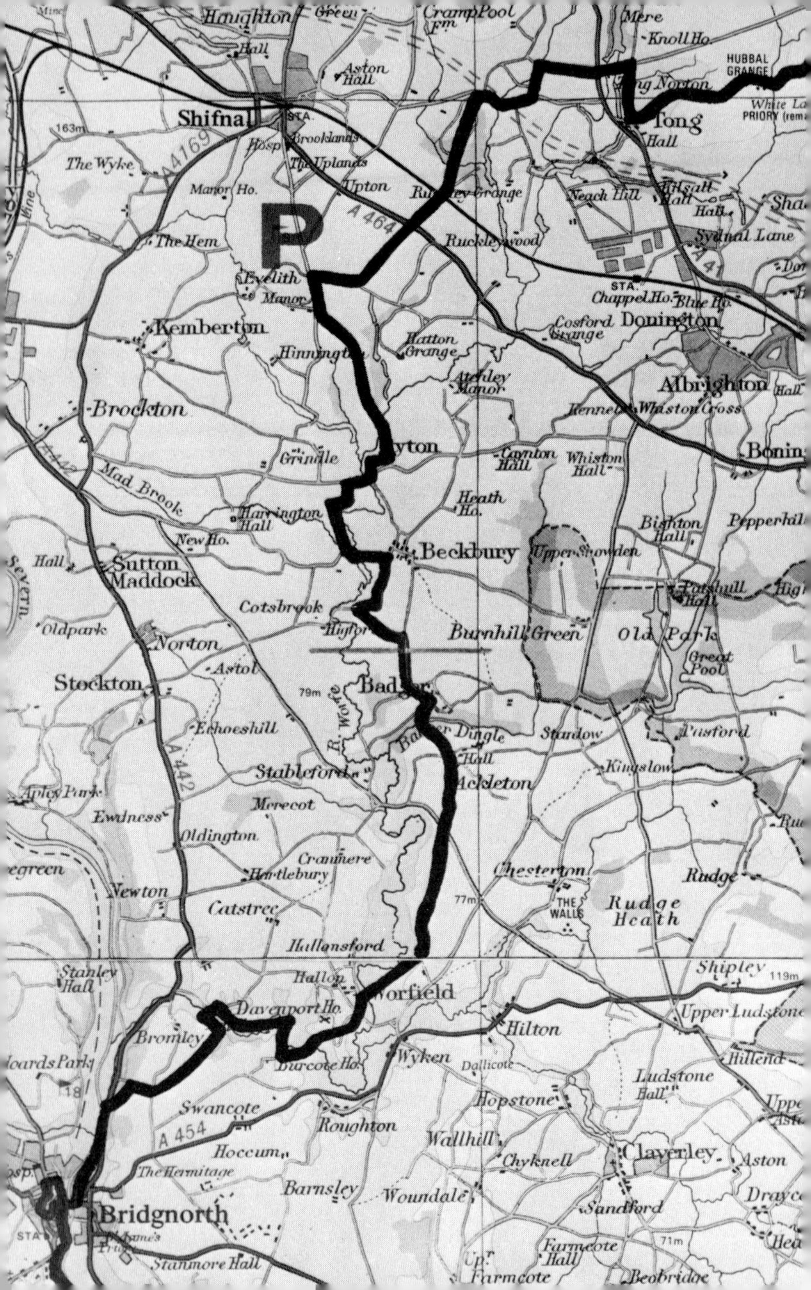

Haughton
Green
Cramp Pool Fm
Mere
Knoll Ho.
Hall
Aston Hall
HUBBAL GRANGE
Shifnal
STA.
163m
A 4169
Hosp
Brooklands
The Uplands
Tong
White La
PRIORY (rem
Hall
The Wyke
Manor Ho.
Upton
A 464
Neach Hill
Hall
Hall
P
The Hem
Ruckleywood
Sydnal Lane
Evelith
Manor
STA.
Chappel Ho.
Blue Ho.
Kemberton
Cosford Grange
Donington
Hatton Grange
Albrighton
Atchley Manor
Hall
Brockton
Kennels
Whiston Cross
Grindle
Whiston Hall
Mad Brook
Heath Ho.
Harrington Hall
Bishton Hall
New Ho.
Beckbury
Upper Snowden
Hall
Sutton Maddock
Patshull Hall
Cotsbrook
Oldpark
Norton
Burnhill Green
Old Park
Great Pool
Stockton
Astol
Badger
79m
R. Worfe
Echoeshill
Badger Dingle
Hall
Stanlow
Pasford
Stableford
Kingslow
Ackleton
Apley Park
Mercot
Ewdness
Oldington
Cranmere
Hartlebury
Chesterton
Rudge
Newton
77m
THE WALLS
Rudge Heath
Catstree
Hallonsford
Stanley Hall
Shipley
119m
Hallon
Worfield
Davenport Ho.
Upper Ludstone
Hilton
Bromley
Burcote Ho.
Wyken
Dallicote
Hillend
Ludstone Hall
Swancote
Hopstone
A 454
Roughton
Wallhill
Hoccum
Claverley
Aston
Chyknell
The Hermitage
Barnsley
Woundale
Bridgnorth
Sandford
STA
71m
Farmcote Hall
Stanmore Hall
Upr Farmcote
Beobridge

7 **Bridgnorth – Worfield – Ackleton – Badger – Beckbury – Ryton – Tong**

Distance: 17½ miles/28·2 km

Cross the bridge over the River Severn in Bridgnorth, and turn left down the steps immediately in front of the clock tower memorial, erected to the memory of two railway engineers, Richard Trevithick and John Rastrick. Walk along the roadway beside the river, noting the good view across to the High Town. Continue along the tarmac path at the end of this roadway, and then walk along the left-hand edge of the recreation ground beside the river. Fort Pendlestone is visible in front. At the end of the recreation ground, cross the fence and continue alongside the pumping station to the end of the path, where it joins the main A442 road.

Continue ahead, and walk along the road between the aptly named High Rock on the right and the river. Immediately after passing Fort Pendlestone, and opposite the end of its buildings, turn up the footpath on the right. This path climbs steeply, initially with a fence on the left and high rock faces on the right; and then as it ascends, it passes through very pleasant woodland. At the top of the climb, arrive alongside the fence on the right running along the top edge of the woodland. The path now continues for a short distance just inside the wood's edge, and then bearing right, passes between two wooden posts. Leaving the woodland, it runs straight ahead between hedges. Note the excellent view across to the left from here. Shortly passing cottages and a farm on the right, the path continues as a hedged track. Arriving at the end of this, turn left along the lane, and then almost immediately right down the track.

After about 400 yards/366 m, continue through the gateway near a small group of houses, and follow the track gently downhill along the bottom of a shallow valley, through an area of heathland. After passing fern-covered slopes on the left, the track turns through a gateway on the right, and then turning left, and now fenced, continues downhill through a

Bridgnorth – Tong

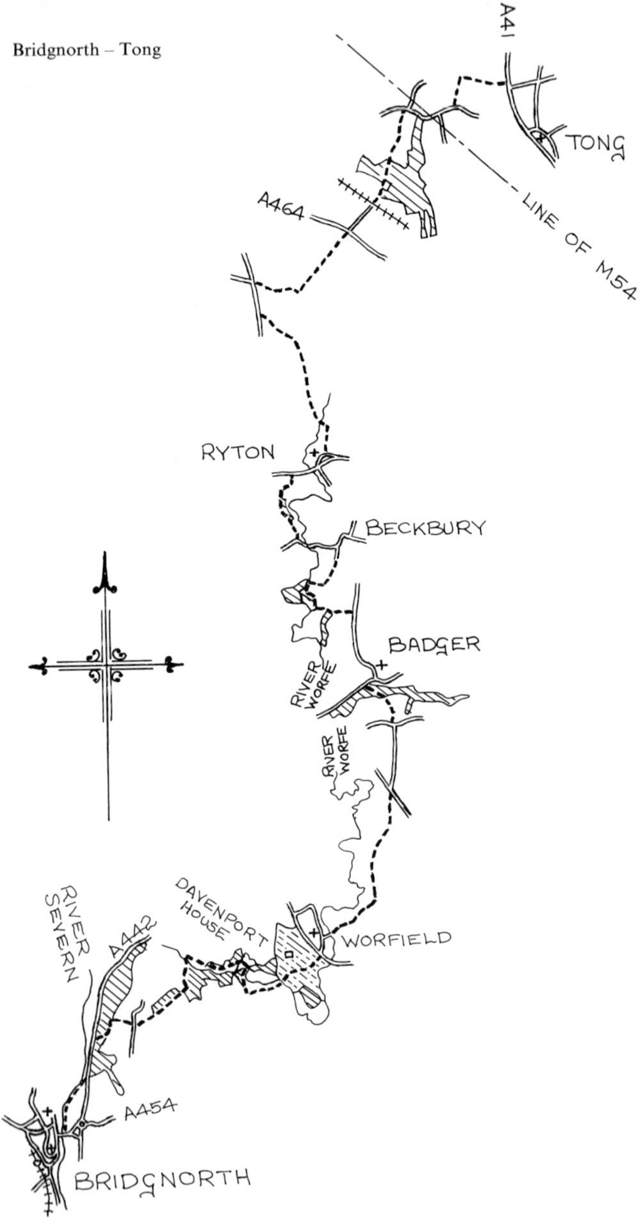

River Worfe and old mill wheel

wooded area. Arriving at the River Worfe, turn left and follow the track along the bank of the river. After about 150 yards/137 m, cross two footbridges in succession, and turning right, a third; and then walk alongside Rindleford Mill on the left.

Turn right immediately after you pass the mill, and walk along the good and partially surfaced track. Cross a cattle-grid near a bend in the river, and continue along this very scenic, well wooded, rock-walled valley. Shortly cross a second cattle-grid, and then after a while, a stone bridge over the river. After about 100 yards/91 m, cross a further cattle-grid alongside a white house. Pass to the right of this house, and shortly go through the gateway in front. Continue along the track, which now bears round to the right alongside a sheer rock face. From this point, the valley now opens out into pleasant pastureland. Go through the gateway at the end of the rock face, and follow the track which now ascends gradually above the river. Immediately after passing a house and its garden on the left, turn sharp left and walk through the gateway between this garden and a barn and other farm buildings. Walk diagonally to the left across the field, and join the track leading out of the farmyard. Follow this as it bears round to the right and leads to the left-hand of the two gateways at the edge of the field. Go through this gateway into the corner of the next field, and walk diagonally to the left across this, heading for a point at its edge which is in line with the gap on the skyline in front, between a wood to the right and the end of a line of trees to the left. Cross the hedge at this point, and continue straight on across the next field to the footbridge over the river. This can be seen about 200 yards/183 m ahead, and to the right of the old mill wheel.

Cross the bridge, and continue straight on across the parkland, heading for the stile just to the right of the gateway that can be seen in front, with a track leading up hill away from it. Davenport House, seen on the skyline across towards the left, was built in 1726 by Francis Smith of Warwick. Cross the stile, and walk up the track in front. At the top of the climb, cross the roadway leading to Davenport House and continue ahead between the two trees with a Scots pine just beyond them. Walk down the slope, heading towards the bungalow that is seen some way in front, midway between the group of houses near the river and a black and white house visible through the trees to the left. At the foot of the slope, recross the Davenport House driveway and then the fence immediately in front. Walk diagonally left to the far corner of the field, noting the old folly on the hillside to the left. Pass through the gateway at the corner, and turning left walk along the left-hand edge of the next field for a few yards to the gateway in front.

Cross straight over the road, and take the lane opposite,

signposted *Worfield*. Follow this into Worfield village, shortly passing the village inn, known both as the Davenport Arms and the Dog. A few yards further on, turn down the lane on the right.

A walk through the village to St Peter's church is a desirable diversion. This fourteenth-century church is set below a wooded cliff, and has an elegant stone spire, rare for Shropshire. Opposite is the seventeenth-century timber-framed Lower Hall.

After a few yards, having returned to your route, pass Mill Close on the right and continue along the track in front,

Entrance to Worfield

noting the beautiful Lower Hall garden behind the wall on the left. Cross the footbridge over the River Worfe, and continue along the track. At the end of this, pass straight over the cross-track and, crossing the cattle-grid, walk along the left-hand edge of the field. Go through the gateway and continue along the left-hand edge of the next field, now in more open countryside. Pass through the gateway, and bearing slightly to the left walk across the following field, keeping parallel to the line of trees on the left, along the top of a steep bank. Continue to the gateway in front, which is on the right of the ash tree and some 50 yards/46 m to the left of the double electricity post in the hedge.

Go through this gateway and, turning towards the left,

Worfield village

walk straight across the field in front to its far corner. The heading for this is to walk towards the point where the field on the right of the dip in the skyline ahead comes down to join the hedge along the bottom of the field on the left. Additionally, the line of your path veers slightly away from a parallel to the electricity line across the field. About three-quarters of the way across this field, cross a temporary fence, and continue to the corner. Cross the fence just to the right of this, and immediately go through the gateway on the left into the corner of the next field. Follow the right-hand edge of this, climbing gently up to its top end. Cross the fence in front, and proceed along the right-hand edge of the next field. Pass through the gateway, and continue along the top edge of the following small field. Cross the fence in front, and walk along the top edge of the next field. Go through the gateway in front, and climb gently up the left-hand edge of the field following. Pass through the gateway, and continue along the left-hand edge of the next field. Ackleton village is now seen in front. Pass through the gateway at the end of the field, and walk along the hedged track. Go through the gateway at the end of this, and continue along the right-hand edge of the field. Go through the gateway and walk down the farm driveway, passing between the farm buildings and the house, to the gateway leading on to the lane. The Folly Inn is a few yards to the right.

Turn left along the lane, and almost immediately right down the lane leading to Ackleton village. Shortly this climbs quite steeply up through the village. Turn left at its end, passing the Red Cow Inn on the right.

Immediately after the cottage next to the inn, turn right down the hedged track. Bear left at the end of this, and follow the left-hand edge of the field for a few yards to the point where the hedge turns away to the left. From here, walk diagonally to the left across the field, to a point alongside the woodland about 50 yards/46 m before the far corner. Continue down the good path into the wooded Badger Dingle. At the bottom, arrive alongside the Upper Pool, and then turn right across the bridge. This spans the stream leading from the pool via an attractive waterfall. Continue across the Dingle and, passing under the bridge carrying one of the Badger Hall driveways, climb up out of the Dingle.

Turn right at the top and walk along the lane, shortly bearing left at the junction in Badger village and passing a large pond on the right. Pass the lane leading to St Giles' church, built in 1834, and then a second pond. The cottage on the left carries an interesting plaque stating that it has been blessed by the Bishop of Shrewsbury.

Continuing round the double bend in the lane, pass a driveway on the left running between two belts of trees. About 500 yards/457 m from this point, pass Badger Farm, and then after a further 350 yards/320 m, turn left just before

St Giles, Badger

reaching the cottages and walk along the hedged track. Continue to the gateway at the end of this, having dropped downhill through the end of a stretch of woodland. Pass through the gateway, and walk straight across the field in front, heading directly towards the large house some way ahead. After passing some 50 yards/46 m to the right of a pond in the field, arrive at the head of a depression running down to the left, with an ash tree at its head. Just after this point, and approximately 75 yards/69 m before reaching the hedge in front, turn right, and walk parallel to this hedge to the intruding field corner. Continue ahead from here, now walking alongside the hedge and fence on the right. Go through the gateway in front, and avoiding the more obvious path which drops steeply away to the left down the wooded depression, bear towards the left and walk along the fairly well defined path which runs just inside and below the top right hand edge of this woodland.

At the end of this stretch of woodland, pass through the remains of a gateway, and arrive at the top corner of a plantation. Turn slightly towards the right, and continue for a few yards to a cross-track. Turn right along this, and immediately pass through a gateway. Follow the track which runs gently uphill, once again just inside the right-hand top edge that we were previously following. At the foot of the steep bank on the left is the River Worfe. Shortly pass through a shallow cutting, and from the head of this continue straight across the middle of the very large field, following the line where a hedge has obviously been removed and keeping parallel to the electricity power lines on the left. Shortly arrive alongside a small pond on the left in a clump of bushes in the middle of the field. Turn left immediately after this, and walk along the good track towards Beckbury village in front, and passing under two sets of power lines. At the end of the field, continue straight on along the roadway in front.

At the end of the roadway turn left along the lane, passing the Seven Stars Inn on the right. Dropping downhill, shortly cross the River Worfe. About 200 yards/183 m after the bridge, and immediately after the two cottages on the left, turn through the gateway on the right and walk straight across the field to the footbridge over the stream in front. Cross this, and initially walking uphill along the left-hand edge of the field, continue straight ahead across it from the point where the fence turns away uphill to the left. The heading is towards the gateway at the far side, which is seen once the low brow in the field has been crossed. Approximately 100 yards/91 m before reaching this gateway, bear left and walk uphill along the top of the steep and fairly well wooded bank dropping away to the right. Cross the fence at the top of the field, and walk along the right-hand edge of the one following, still along the top of the bank. Good views are seen down to the right across the valley of the River Worfe. Near the end of the bank, cross the fence in front and continue straight on over the next field, keeping parallel to the fence and hedge across to the left. Arriving at the fence and hedge in front, at the head of the depression running up from the river valley, turn right, and walk alongside the hedge on the left. After a short distance, turn through the first gateway on the left, and walk along the fenced and hedged track.

At the end of the track, turn right along the lane, which shortly drops downhill to cross the River Worfe. Just over the bridge, turn left opposite the lane to Beckbury, and walk up the dirt road through Ryton village. Passing the eighteenth-century church at the top of the climb, walk along the tarmac road for about 150 yards/137 m to the gateway on the left immediately after the farm buildings and house.

Turn through the gateway, and walk along the left-hand edge of the field. Go through the gateway in front after passing the farm complex, and continue down the fenced track at the bottom of a shallow cutting. Just before reaching the gateway directly in front, turn sharp left and continue with the track to cross Adamsford Bridge over the river. The track now bears right, and climbing gently uphill, passes a wood on the right. Continue on to the end of the track (approximately 1 mile/1·6 km) passing Hatton Grange Farm on the right, at which point the surface becomes tarmac. Turn right at the end, and walk along the lane.

After just over a ¼-mile/400 m, and opposite the first lane on the left, turn through the opening on the right and follow the track along the right-hand edge of the field towards Nursery Cottage. At the end of the field, continue along the hedged and fenced track, and after about 100 yards/91 m follow the footpath alongside the hedge on the right, across the front of the garden to the house. After a few yards, veer slightly to the left, and passing through the opening in the fence in front, walk along the path between a small stretch of woodland and a hedge.

Arriving at the cross-track leading from Twybrook Cottage on the right; turn left, and walk the length of this good straight, hedged and fenced track to its end (approximately ¾-mile/1·2 km), noting the stump of an old windmill on the skyline to the left. Cross straight over the main A464 road, and follow the tarmac roadway opposite. Continue along the track in front where this finishes, crossing Bonemill Bridge over the Wolverhampton–Shrewsbury railway-line. After about 175 yards/160 m, and just after passing through a gateway, fork left at the junction, following the track which shortly runs through a pleasant area of woodland. After leaving this, continue for about a ½-mile/800 m to the end of the hedged track.

At this point, the projected route of the M54 motorway crosses our path. A description of the revised walk here is given after the next paragraph.

Until the motorway is built, the walk continues as follows: Pass through the gateway at the end of the track, and turning right walk down the lane, passing Lizard Lane on the left, to cross Timlet Bridge over the river at the bottom of the slope. Shortly, pass a lane on the right signposted *Neachley*, and after approximately a further 220 yards/201m, turn left along the track immediately before the stretch of woodland.

When the motorway is built, the walk is as follows: At the end of the track, turn right along the lane, immediately passing a lane on the right leading down to Timlet Bridge and Neachley. After a few yards pass beneath the motorway, and then pass the realigned Lizard Lane on the left. After approximately 500 yards/457 m, turn left along the track.

Both routes now continue as follows: Walk along the hedged track, which continues as a concrete roadway, to a small factory. Bear left here and follow the track downhill, now with a dirt surface. Just before reaching the bottom and the bridge across the stream, turn sharp right, and walk back uphill along a second track, climbing fairly steeply. Note the unusual little square house on the left here, with interesting brickwork patterning in its walls. From the top of the climb, continue on to the gateway at the end of the track.

St Bartholomew's, Tong

Pass through the gateway, and turn right for a few yards along the main A41 road, and then, opposite the Bell Inn, turn left down the lane signposted *Bishops Wood.* Follow this lane for a ¼-mile/400 m, and turn right at the crossroads in Tong Norton, towards Albrighton. Walk the length of the lane to its finish at the junction opposite St Bartholomew's church, Tong.

This magnificent church has been described as the village Westminster Abbey. Dating from the fifteenth-century, it contains a wealth of monuments, carving, gilding, and painting. There are bullet marks on the north door and wall, reminding us that the Civil War passed this way. In his book *The Old Curiosity Shop*, Charles Dickens modelled his church and village on Tong, and it does not take much imagination to see Little Nell seated amongst the monuments here. St Bartholomew's was originally a collegiate church, and on the slope below it the remains of the medieval college can be seen.

From the junction, turn left and walk the few yards into the little village of Tong.

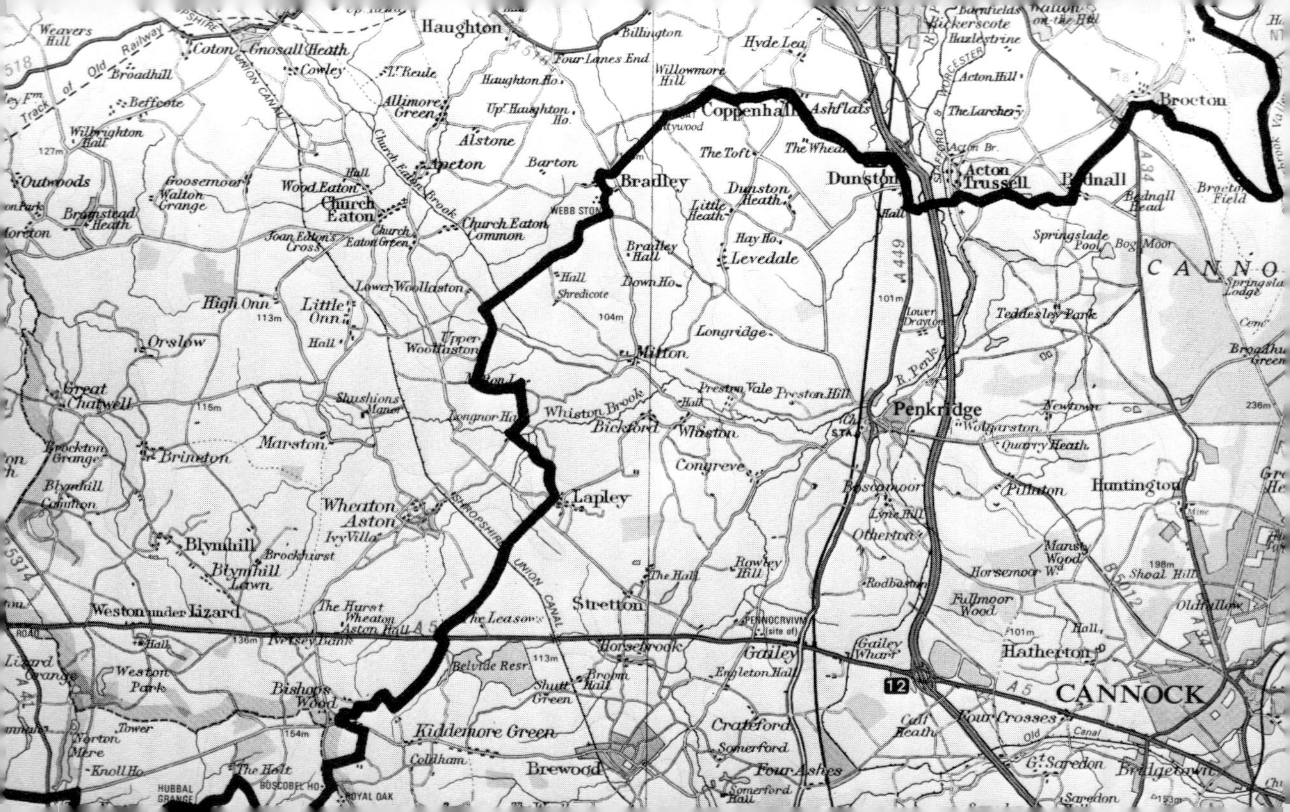

Haughton
Billington
Hyde Lea
Brocton
Weavers Hill
Coton
Gnosall Heath
Cowley
Broadhill
Beffcote
Wilbrighton Hall
Outwoods
Goosemoor
Walton Grange
Bromstead Heath
Wood Eaton
Church Eaton
Church Eaton Common
Joan Eaton's Cross
Church Eaton Green
Church Eaton Brook
Allimore Green
Apeton
Alstone
Barton
Four Lanes End
Haughton Ho.
Upr Haughton Ho.
Willowmore Hill
Coppenhall
Ashflats
The Toft
Bradley
Webb Stone
Dunston
Dunston Heath
Little Heath
Hay Ho.
Levedale
Bradley Hall
Down Ho.
Shredicote
Acton Trussell
Acton Hill
The Larchery
Bickerscote
Hazlestrine
Bednall
Bednall Head
Brocton Field
Springslade Pool
Bog Moor
Springslade Lodge
Teddesley Park
CANNOCK
Broadhurst Green
High Onn
Little Onn
Lower Woollaston
Upper Woollaston
Orslow
Great Chatwell
Shushions Manor
Longridge
Milton
Preston Vale
Preston Hill
Lower Drayton
R. Penk
Penkridge
Newtown
Wolgarston
Quarry Heath
Whiston Brook
Bickford
Whiston
Congreve
Longnor Ho.
Marston
Brineton
Brockton Grange
Blymhill Common
Blymhill
Blymhill Lawn
Brockhurst
Wheaton Aston
Ivy Villa
Lapley
Shropshire Union Canal
Rowley Hill
The Hall
Stretton
Pillaton
Huntington
Boscomoor
Lyne Hill
Otherton
Rodbaston
Horsemoor Wd
Mansty Wood
Shoal Hill
Fullmoor Wood
Weston under Lizard
The Hurst
Wheaton Aston Hall
The Leasows
Pennocrvivm (site of)
Horsebrook
Gailey
Gailey Wharf
Hatherton
Lizard Grange
Weston Park
Bishops Wood
Belvide Resr
Brom Hall
Shutt Green
Engleton Hall
Kiddemore Green
Crateford
Somerford
Calf Heath
Four Crosses
Norton Mere
Tower
Knoll Ho.
Codsall
The Holt
Hubbal Grange
Boscobel Ho.
Royal Oak
Brewood
Four Ashes
Somerford Hall
Gt Saredon
Bridgetown
Saredon
A 5
A 34
A 449
A 41
B 5012
12

8 **Tong – Boscobel – Bishops Wood – Lapley – Longnor – Bradley – Coppenhall – Dunston – Acton Trussell – Bednall – Brocton**

Distance: 19½ miles/31·4 km

From Tong village take the lane on the left. After about 600 yards/549 m pass Tong Hill Farm on the left at the lane end, and continue straight on along the hedged track in front. Good views are to be seen across to the left and slightly behind. After some distance pass the remains of Hubbal Grange on the right. This ruined timber-framed building was the home of Richard Penderel, who was instrumental in hiding King Charles II on his flight from the Battle of Worcester and in helping him escape to France.

Passing through a gateway, continue on along the track which climbs gently for its last few yards to finish at a tarmac roadway. Continue straight on along this, and passing through a gateway, turn sharp right and walk along the roadway to its finish at Meashill Farm. Extensive views across to the right include the Wrekin and beyond. Arriving in front of the farmhouse, turn though the gateway on the left, and walk diagonally to the right across the farmyard. Passing through the small wicket gate, walk straight across the poultry yard, and then go through a second wicket gate. (In passing through this farm, the route is that recommended to us by the farmer, and is not the definitive path which runs round to the right of the complex.)

Turn left here along the end of a small field, and almost immediately, passing through the gateway in front, turn right and walk along the right-hand edge of the field. Go through the gateway, and continue straight on along the left-hand edge of the next field. Pass through the small gate at the end of this, and follow the wooded path. In the field on the right near the end of this, is the ruin of White Ladies Priory. This late-Norman building was the home of Augustinian nuns. Pass through the gate at the end of the path and continue along the wooded track in front. Go through the gateway at the end of this, and turn left along the lane.

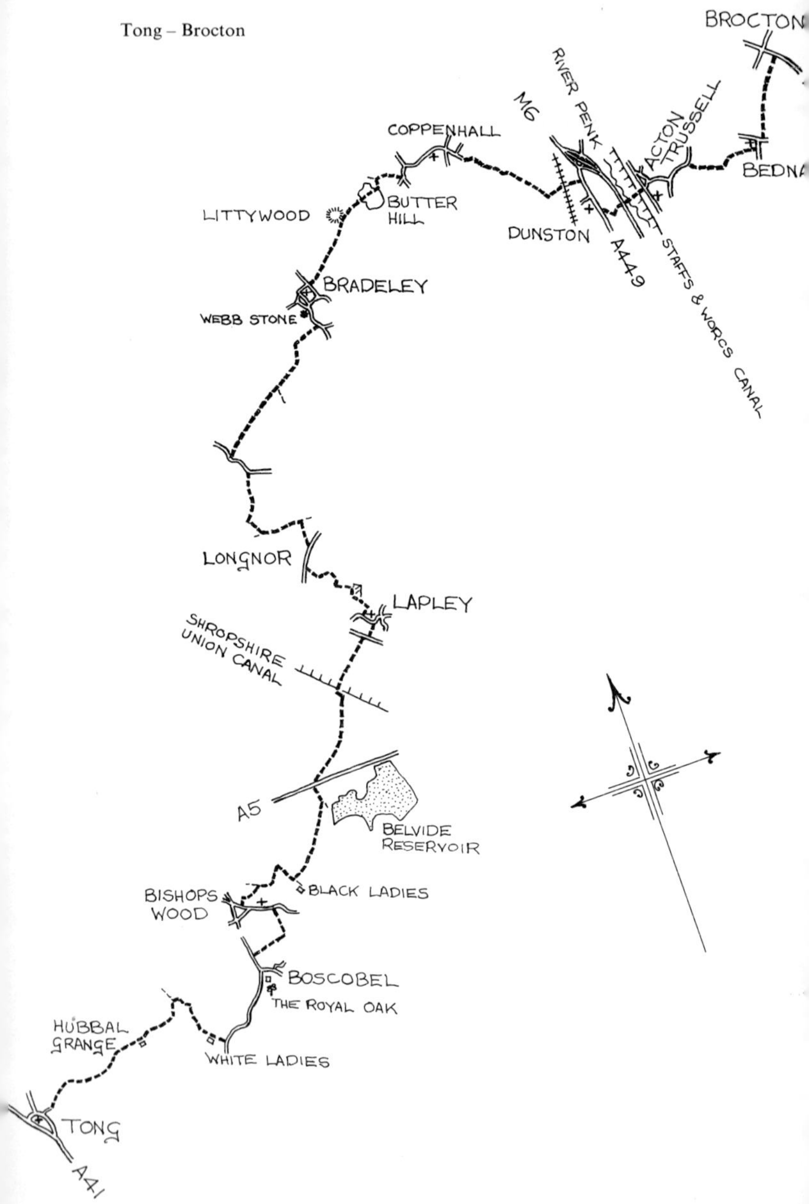
BROCTON
RIVER PENK
M6
ACTON TRUSSELL
COPPENHALL
BEDNA
BUTTER HILL
LITTYWOOD
DUNSTON
A449
STAFFS & WORCS CANAL
BRADELEY
WEBB STONE
LONGNOR
LAPLEY
SHROPSHIRE UNION CANAL
A5
BELVIDE RESERVOIR
BLACK LADIES
BISHOPS WOOD
BOSCOBEL
THE ROYAL OAK
HUBBAL GRANGE
WHITE LADIES
TONG
A41

Hubbal Grange
White Ladies Priory

The lane climbs gently uphill, and Boscobel House is soon seen in front. Just before reaching the house, the Royal Oak can be seen in the middle of the field on the right. This tree, formerly surrounded by woodland, was the hiding-place for King Charles II when he was being sought by Cromwell's soldiers, following his defeat at the Battle of Worcester. The King spent two September days at Boscobel in that year of 1651, staying hidden in one of the numerous priest's hiding-places in the house.

Pass Boscobel House, and turn left at the T-junction. Walk down the lane, which here forms the boundary between Shropshire and Staffordshire, and after approximately 300 yards/274 m, and immediately before the house, turn right

The Royal Oak, Boscobel

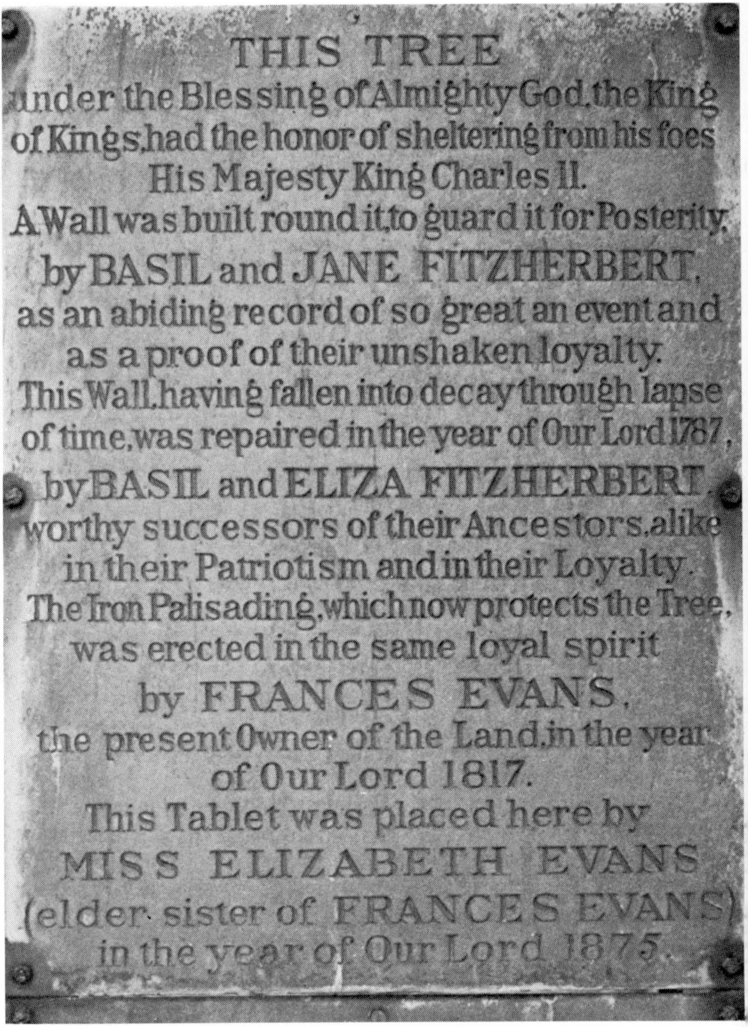

Notice on the Royal Oak

along the hedged track. Immediately after Pearse Hay Farm on the right, turn sharp left and continue to the end of the track.

Turn left here and walk along the lane, passing Bishops Wood church on the right. About 200 yards/183 m after the church, bear right with the lane at the fork, and then after a further 100 yards/91 m, turn right up the tarmac roadway. Bear right with this after approximately 140 yards/128 m, and pass Church Farm on the right. Continue down the hedged track at the end of the roadway, and at the bottom of the slope bear right along the cross-track. This shortly climbs fairly steeply. Arriving at Top Barn Farm, turn right with the track, passing the farm buildings on the left. At the bottom of

Black Ladies

the first field after these buildings, turn through the gateway on the left into this field. However, first note Black Ladies, the large house about 150 yards/137 m further along the track. This is built on the site of a Norman convent of black-robed nuns.

Walk along the edge of the field alongside the hedge on the right. Go through the gateway, and continue along the right-hand edge of the next field. Just before the end of this field, note the interesting pool on the right, the home of innumerable waterfowl. At the end of the field pass through the gateway just to the left of the corner, and walk straight across the following field, heading for a point just to the right of the electricity post, seen in the hedgerow beyond the opposite edge of the field. Belvide Reservoir is across to the right, and on the skyline beyond are the woodlands of Cannock Chase, with the Post Office Tower prominent. Cross the fence alongside the oak tree, and continue ahead in the same direction, across the corner of the next field, shortly passing near to the hedge on the left. Cross the fence in front, about 50 yards/46 m to the right of the field corner, and continue on across the following field, heading towards the cottage some way beyond. Cross the fence in front some yards to the right of the depression, and continue straight across the next field to the gateway seen just to the right of the cottage. In season this field is carpeted with a profusion of tiny wild pansies. Pass through the gateway, and turning left walk along the good track.

Turn left at the end of the track, and walk for a few yards along the main A5 road, and then turn through the first gateway on the right, just before White Gate Farm, following the signpost *Public Footpath–Wheaton Aston.* Walk along the short hedged track, passing the farm complex on the left, and continue alongside the hedge on the right to the gateway in front. Pass through this, or cross the cattle-grid, and follow the track along the right-hand edge of the field. Continue through the gateway and walk along the right-hand edge of the next field. Wheaton Aston village is seen across to the left.

After some distance, pass a pond on the right just behind the hedge, and then approximately 100 yards/91 m further on, where the field narrows to a neck about 50 yards/46 m wide, turn left and walk across this neck to the stile at the intruding field corner.

Cross this stile into the corner of the next field, and walk along its right-hand edge. Cross the fence, and almost immediately turn through the small gate on the right. Turn left and walk along the very short fenced section, and then cross the fence in front. Initially, walk between the hedge on the right and a fence on the left, at the narrow end of the next field, and then after a few yards follow the fence and hedge on the left, walking amongst the narrow belt of oaks running part-way along this edge of the field. Pass through the gateway, and bearing left walk alongside the hedge in the small field, leading round into a hedged track. Walk along this for about 70 yards/64 m, and then turn right along the short track leading to the gateway at the end of the bridge over the Shropshire Union Canal, which here runs through a pleasant wooded cutting. Cross the bridge, and continue along the track leading to Lapley Wood Farm. Pass through the farmyard, and then through the gateway in front. Passing the farmhouse on the right, walk along the hedged farm roadway. Lapley Church can now be seen in front.

At the end of the roadway, turn right along the old lane for a few yards, and then turn through the gateway on the left just before the houses. Walk up the right-hand edge of the field, heading for Lapley Church. Go through the gateway and turn left along the lane. Lapley village and the Vaughan Arms Inn are along to the right. Lapley Church dates mainly from the fifteenth century, but it has a Norman base to the tower.

Immediately past the church, turn through the gateway on the right, and walking to the end of the tarmac driveway pass through the gateway just to the left of the garage of Lapley Manor. Walk alongside the iron railings on the left-hand edge of the field, and, passing through the gateway, walk along the left-hand edge of the next field. Extensive views are seen across to the right, to Cannock Chase on the skyline. At the end of this field, go through the gateway on the left at the corner, and walk along the edge of the next field, with Pool Plantation, a small coppice, on the right. At the corner of the plantation, turn right across the fence, and walk for a few yards along the end of the plantation; and then, passing through the remains of a gateway, turn left. Almost immediately, cross the fence in front, and walk along the left-hand edge of the field. Just before reaching the pond in a clump of trees, cross the fence in front, and passing to the left of this pond, keep alongside the hedge and fence. Cross the fence in front, back into the same field as before.

From this point, bear slightly towards the right, and walk straight across the field towards the small gateway that can be seen at the field bottom, about 250 yards/229 m to the right of the corner. Cross the stream and, passing through the gate, walk straight ahead across the next field to the oak tree at the opposite side—just to the left of the large house some way beyond. Just before reaching this tree, cross the fence into the corner of the right-hand of the two following fields. Walk diagonally across this, to the stile at the opposite side. Cross the stile, and continue on across the next field, to cross the fence alongside an oak tree at the far side. In crossing this field, pass to the left of a pond and to the right of an electricity pole. Walk across the following field, still in the same direction, to the gateway that can be seen at the opposite side just to the left of an intruding field corner. From this corner, walk alongside the hedge on the right, to the gateway. Pass through this, and turning right, walk along the lane through the hamlet of Longnor.

Cross the bridge over Longnor Brook, and after approximately 200 yards/183m, pass Longnor Hall Farm on the right. About 50 yards/46 m after the farm complex, turn through the gateway on the left and walk diagonally towards the right across the field to its far corner, heading towards the cottage on the skyline some way beyond. Cross the fence in

the corner, and immediately turn through the gateway on the left. Continue diagonally to the right across the next field, heading for a point some 100 yards/91 m to the left of the cottage. Go through the small gate in the hedge and, turning left, walk along the hedged and slightly wooded track.

Reaching the end of the fourth field on the right along the track, turn through the gateway into the corner of this same field. Walk away from the track along the left-hand edge of the field, following the line of telegraph poles. Go through the gateway, and continue alongside the fence on the left, across the small enclosure. Almost immediately cross the fence in front, and walk along the left-hand edge of the next field, still with the line of telegraph poles. Cannock Chase can be seen over to the right. Cross the fence, and continue along the left-hand edge of the following field. At the end of this, cross the fence and continue ahead along the fenced track, passing a farm on the left. Go through the gateway in front and walk down the hedged track. At the end of this, turn left along the lane.

After approximately 400 yards/366 m, turn through the gateway on the right (or cross the stile) opposite the white cottage at the bend in the lane. Walk along the right-hand edge of the field. Cross the ditch and stile, and continue along the right-hand edge of the next field. At the end of this, cross the gated footbridge over Church Eaton Brook, and walk along the left-hand edge of the field. Pass through the gateway at the end of this and continue along the left-hand edge of the next. Go through the gateway, and walk along the left-hand edge of the following field, passing a pond on the right about halfway along. Pass through the gateway just short of the end of the field, and continue ahead along the hedged track. Just before its end, the track turns right to join a cross-track. Turn left and walk along this second hedged track to its end (about $\frac{3}{4}$-mile/1·2 km).

Turn left, and walk along the lane to Bradley village. Just before bearing left at the fork, note the Webb Stone on the left

The Webb Stone, Bradley

outside the gates of a house named Lyndhurst. A local legend relating to this stone states that all maidens passing by should bow to the stone, thus avoiding the fate of remaining spinsters for the rest of their lives. Pass the Post Office on the left and continue through the village. The Red Lion Inn and the church of St Mary and All Saints are on the right. This very pretty church, some 500 years old, is practically covered by virginia creeper.

Turn right around the church, and follow the lane to its end at a T-junction. Continue straight over this junction, and go through the gateway opposite. Walk along the left-hand edge of the small field, and cross the fence in the corner amongst the bushes. Heading slightly to the left from here, walk diagonally across the next field to the gateway in the far

In Bradley Village

corner. Go through this gateway and continue along the left-hand edge of the following field. A track runs immediately behind the hedge on the left. Cross the fence, and walk along the left-hand edge of the long narrow field. At the end of this cross the stile, ditch, and fence, and continue along the left-hand edge of the next field, heading towards Butter Hill which is prominent in front. Go through the gateway and walk ahead along the track, alongside the farm buildings on the right.

An interesting and unusual double circular moat lies behind the hedge on the left. A house named Littywood now stands in the centre. In some sections the outer moat still contains water, and one such section is seen a few yards further on, alongside a track which leads off to the left.

Continue through the gateway in front, alongside the farmyard, and follow the fence on the left, passing two Dutch barns on the right. After a few yards go through the gateway and continue ahead, shortly climbing gently up Butter Hill, following the right-hand edge of the field. Cross the fence into the corner of the next field, near the top of the hill. Good wide panoramic views are seen from here, with Stafford towards the left and the ruins of its castle prominent on top of a hill.

Walk diagonally to the left across the field, heading for a point at its far side just to the left of the trees in the hedgerow. After a few yards, and having reached the brow of the field, a gate can be seen in front. Cross the fence immediately to the left of this gate, and directly in line with the telegraph pole. Turn left and walk along the track for about 35 yards/32 m, to the left-hand bend. Turn right here and cross the fence into the field. Walk across this, bearing slightly towards the right, and heading directly for the left hand of the two treetops that can be seen above the skyline. Once the brow of the field has been crossed, the bearing leads directly into the corner in front. Cross the fence here, and continue diagonally across the corner of the next field, to the gateway in the hedge a short way in front. Note the stump of an old windmill across to the right, and the excellent panoramic views of Cannock Chase in front. Go through the gateway, and walk diagonally across the next field, heading for a point just to the right of the house beyond the brow of the field, and directly in line with the Post Office Tower which is prominent on Cannock Chase. Having crossed the field brow, a gateway is seen in front to the right of the house. Go through this gateway, and turning left, walk along the lane.

After a short distance, turn right at the junction signposted *Coppenhall.* Follow this lane to Coppenhall village, passing the perfect little thirteenth-century church of St Lawrence on the right. Continue straight over the junction at the end of the lane, and take the lane directly opposite. After a short distance, pass Beech Lane on the left. A few yards further on, continue along the track in front that runs downhill between hedges. After the double bend, pass through the gateway and continue for some distance to the Dutch barn at the end of the track. Pass to the left of this, and walk straight across the field in front, heading directly towards the spire of Dunston Church, about 1 mile/1·6 km away.

After crossing the field, the heading brings you to an intruding field corner. Go through the small gate at this point, and walk diagonally across the end of the next field, to the intruding corner in front coming from the right. Continue on, diagonally from this corner, across the remainder of this very large field, now heading for an electricity pole seen some way before a railway bridge, to the right of the church spire. Arriving at the electricity pole, cross the field bridge on its left, over a small stream, and bearing to the left of your previous heading, walk straight across the next field keeping parallel to the electricity power line, to arrive at another bridge over the railway. Cross this gated bridge, spanning the main Wolverhampton–Stafford line, and walk along the left-hand edge of the field. The M6 motorway, which has been visible for some while, is now prominent over to the left. Cross the fence and turn right along the concrete roadway, almost immediately passing through a gateway, and continue down the slope. Just before the bottom of this, turn through the gateway on the left on to the main A449 road.

Turning right, walk along the road through Dunston village, passing the nineteenth-century church of St Leonard on the right. Continue along the main road, and after some yards pass Dunston Hall on the right. About 25 yards/23 m after passing the Hall, turn through the wicket gate in the hedge on the left and walk diagonally to the right, down to the far corner of the field. Cross the fence here and, turning towards the left, walk diagonally across the next field, heading for the bridge under the M6 motorway running on its embankment in front, and with Acton Trussell village on the hill beyond. This heading brings you to a fenced intruding field corner. Cross the fence here, and continue diagonally across the next field to the bridge. (From the wicket gate the more obvious direct path across two stiles to this bridge, is unfortunately not the definitive route.) Walk under this bridge below the motorway, and continue along the track in front. After a few yards cross the gated concrete bridge over the River Penk, and continue along the fenced track. After approximately 250 yards/229 m this crosses Acton Moat Bridge over the Staffordshire and Worcestershire Canal. The track now continues between farm buildings, and ends at a gateway leading on to Lower Penkridge Road in Acton Trussell village.

Turn right and walk along the road for a few yards, and then turn left at the first junction into Barn End Road, signposted *Acton Hill* and *Bednall*. The small church of St James, with its Decorated nave and chancel and thirteenth-century tower, is seen some distance further on along Lower Penkridge Road, some way from the village. Note also Acton Moat on the right of this same road. After a few yards, fork right at the telephone kiosk into the lane signposted *Bednall* and *Brocton*. Follow this lane to the end, passing the Post Office on the right, and turn left at the T-junction. Walk along the lane, signposted *Bednall, Brocton*, and *Milford*, for approximately 400 yards/366 m, to the end of the first field on the right.

Turn through the gateway on the right here, and walk along the track leading to Plashes Farm. This first bears left and crosses a small stream, and then bears right, heading for the farm in front. Immediately after the second telegraph pole from the right-hand bend, turn through the gateway on the left into the field. Walk diagonally to the right across this field to the far corner, heading to the left of the electricity pole in the field, itself to the left of the Post Office Tower on Cannock Chase beyond. Cross a temporary fence about halfway over this field, and continue to the stile just to the left of the corner. Cross this stile, the footbridge over the stream, and the old gate immediately after the bridge, into the corner of the next field. Walk along the right-hand edge of this, alongside the partially grubbed-out hedge. Go through the gateway and, bearing right, continue along the right-hand edge of the next field. The spire of Bednall church is seen in front. Pass through the next gateway and continue along the right-hand edge of the following field to a point approximately midway; and then bearing very slightly to the left, walk directly to the gateway ahead, a short distance to the left of the corner. Pass through this and immediately turn through the gateway on its right (at the end of a short track), and then immediately turning through another gateway on the left, walk along a hedged and rather overgrown track. Near its end this track is clear, with a tarmac surface. Turn left at the end.

Follow the lane to its end at the T-junction in Bednall village, with its nineteenth-century church of All Saints on the left. Turn right here, and almost immediately cross the fence on the left at the end of the bungalow garden. Walk along the path beside the garden, alongside a stone wall on the right, and after a few yards cross a stile, and then shortly a second. Walk along the right-hand edge of the field. Immediately after the farm building on the right, turn right with the hedge and cross the fence in front into the corner of the next field. Turn left, and walk along the left-hand edge of this; and passing through the gateway, continue along the left-hand edge of the next one. The good views seen across to the left from here include Stafford, Coppenhall, and the Wrekin.

Cross the ditch and stile at the end of the field, and continue straight on across the next field to the stile in front. Cross this, and walk straight over the following field to the gateway at the opposite side. Go through this gateway, and continue across the next field, heading towards the tops of the houses which can just be seen over the field brow, some distance to the right of the prominent oak tree. The end of Cannock Chase can now be seen across to the right. Having crossed the brow of the field, a second oak tree is seen at the bottom of the slope in front, just before the hedge. Pass to the left of this oak, and cross the stile and small stream into the right-hand of the two following fields. Walk along the left-hand edge of this field, and cross the fence in front. Continue straight on along the left-hand edge of the next field, and crossing the fence walk along the left-hand edge of the following one. Go through the gateway, and walk the few yards alongside the Chetwynd Arms Inn to the main A34 road on the outskirts of Brocton.

Ingestre
Pasturefields
R. Trent
Hall
Lit Ingestre
Lion Lo.
Farley
Swansmoor
Tolldish
Blithfield Resr.
BLITHFIELD HALL
Oakfields
Admaston
Moreton
Lea Hall Fm.
Tixall
Shugborough
Great Haywood
126m
Coley
B 5013
Up. Moreton
New
NT
Shugborough Park
Little Haywood
Hamley Ho.
Stockwell Heath
Milford
COLWICH JN.
Colwich
Bishton Hall
Colton
Haywood Park
NT
Nature Trails
A 513
Haywood
Wolseley
Hall
A 51
Warren
Parchfield Ho.
Brocton
68m
Colton
STA.
Sherbrook Valley
DANGER ZONE
Parks Ho.
Hagley Hall
Cawardens
Brocton Field
Bednall Head
Stonehouse
RUGELEY
Power Sta.
Slitting Mill
A 513
Bog Moor
Nature Trail
209
A 460
A 51
Springslade Lodge
Fairoak Lodge
Brereton
Chetwynds Coppice
Breretonhill
CANNOCK CHASE
Broadhurst Green
Brindley Valley
FOREST
Brindley Heath
Mine
236m
Goods Line
Wandon
Upper Lo
Pye Green
Sukers Lo.
Beaudesert
Rawnsley Hills
118
Old Park
Green Heath
Huntington
Hazelslade
FORT
Mine
Chestall
Mine
Hednesford
Rawnsley
Cannock Wood
High Town
Gentleshaw
198m
Church Hill
Shoal Hill
Littleworth
Goosemoor Green
B 5012
Oldfallow
Wimblebury
A 34
Mine
B 4154
Heath Hayes
Chase Terrace
Boney Hay
CANNOCK
A 5190
179m
Mine
Mine
Burntwood
Leacroft
A 5190
Norton East
Mine
Spring Hill
Bridgetown
Old Canal
B 4154

9 **Cannock Chase including Shugborough and Great Haywood**

Distance: 17½ miles/28·2 km

From the Chetwynd Arms Inn at Brocton, cross the main A34 road and walking along the narrow hedged footpath opposite (to the right of the row of houses) enter the bounds of Cannock Chase. Cross the stile at the end of the rear garden of a house, and continue along the hedged path running behind the gardens of more houses. Cross the next stile and walk along the left-hand edge of the field. Just short of the end of this, and immediately after the farm buildings on the left, turn right just before the footbridge over the concrete channelled stream. Walk gently up the field beside this stream, and some way in front, where the stream drops over a small weir, continue straight on alongside the fence and hedge on the left. Cross the stile and then, after a few yards, turn left over the concrete footbridge. Immediately cross the stile and walk along the narrow path between the bungalow gardens in Brocton village.

At the end of the path turn right along the lane for a few yards, and then almost immediately turn left up the steep hedged track just after the electricity pole. Climbing this track, pass through the hedge, and continue up Tar Hill. Nearing the top of the climb, bear gradually round towards the right and follow the right-hand edge of the higher and flatter area of the top of the hill, keeping the houses down to the right just in view. The excellent panorama across to the right includes The Wrekin and the Clee Hills. Your path now becomes better defined, and runs round the head of a depression sloping down to the houses below. Arriving approximately above the last of these houses, turn left with the more well defined path. Follow this as it winds along the edge of Oldacre Valley, down to the right. Hereabouts the Chase is covered with fern, gorse, heather, and rather scrubby woodland. Some way across to the right the Post Office Tower is prominent over the trees.

After some distance, continue straight ahead across the end

Cannock Chase and Great Haywood

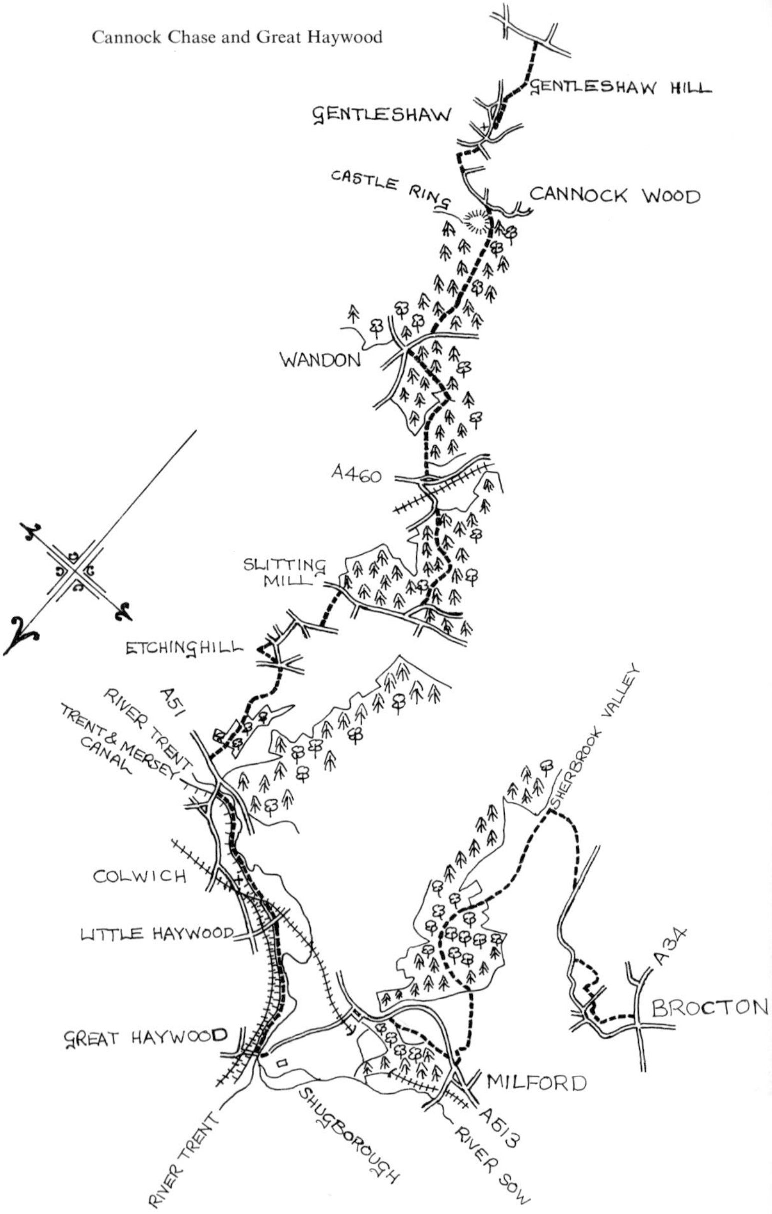

of a track running to the left, and a few yards further on join a good track coming from the left. Almost immediately bear left off this track and, crossing an open area, walk down a short track to join the tarmac roadway running along the edge of the quarry in front.

Turning right, walk along the roadway, noting the unusual form that erosion has created out of the far side of the quarry. The roadway climbs gently uphill, and shortly passes a good track leading off to the left. Approximately 650 yards/594 m after this track, and shortly before the Glacial Boulder on its plinth to the left of the roadway (with a trigonometrical point just beyond) fork left into a small area of open grassland. Go on, passing to the left of the Glacial Boulder and trig point, and join a track running parallel to the roadway. Almost immediately take the left-hand fork and follow this track, noting the marshy area on the right known as Womere. Shortly bear left at the next fork, alongside Womere, and follow the track down into the Sherbrook Valley.

Soon the track ends, and continues as a footpath. Just

Sherbrook Valley

before reaching the Sherbrook stream in the valley, and with woodland beyond, turn left along the main valley path. Follow this, and after some distance cross a tiny brooklet running down from the left. A silver birch can be used as a bridge at this spot. After a short distance, pass an old pumphouse and Lower Sherbrook Pool on the right. Continue along the path in front, which leads into a more wooded area consisting mainly of silver birch and alder. Continue ahead where a track from the right crosses the stream by stepping stones, and walk alongside the fence on the right, beyond which is National Trust land—part of the Shugborough estate. Harts Hill is the pine-covered rise on the right. Pass through the fence and walk the few yards to the end of the track, where it joins a cross-track.

Continue straight over the cross-track and climb the steep path up Oat Hill. Pass to the right of the summit with its few Scots pines and, continuing ahead, descend the opposite side of the hill, heading towards the large building some way below. The River Sow gently winds its way through the delightful panorama in front. At the bottom of the slope, near a pond in a hollow to the left, turn right up the track between Oat Hill and Spring Hill. Arriving on top of the saddle between the two hills, turn left and climb the steep path up to the top of Spring Hill. Once again you are greeted by excellent views. Continue over the summit, following the path which initially heads towards the road junction seen beyond Milford Common at the foot of the hill. After a short distance, bear right and drop steeply downhill beside the fence on the left. At the bottom of the slope, arrive at the main A513 road opposite the main entrance to the National Trust property of Shugborough Hall and its park. A short distance to the left in Milford village is the Barley Mow Inn, and the Little Fawn restaurant and café.

Cross the main road, and turning right, walk along the road for a short distance, following the boundary wall on the left. Turn left with the wall opposite the Milford milestone, and

Triumphal Arch, Shugborough

follow the path gently up through the woodland of Satnall Hills. At the top of the climb, alongside the covered reservoir on the left bear slightly towards the right along the track over the summit, and then drop gently downhill. The pine-covered Harts Hill is prominent across to the right. During the descent, pass over several cross-tracks.

Turn left at the bottom and walk along the main A513 road for approximately 500 yards/457 m. Ignoring the exit roadway from Shugborough Park, turn into the first lane on the left. A notice announces that this is *No Through Road for Motor Vehicles*. Follow this lane, shortly crossing the Lichfield–Stafford railway-line. Note the east entrance to Shugborough Tunnel along to the left, and above and beyond it the Triumphal Arch, one of the many follies in the grounds of Shugborough; the tunnel itself was constructed to ensure that the park remained unspoiled. On the right of the lane here is the Loco Shed—part of the Staffordshire County Museum, which has its home at Shugborough—containing much to delight railway enthusiasts.

Following the lane, cross a cattle-grid and shortly pass the Tower Of The Winds, a second folly, on the left. Continuing along the lane, the full façade of Shugborough Hall comes into view on the left. The home of the Earls of Lichfield, Shugborough Hall dates from 1693, with later additions notably those by Samuel Wyatt around 1800. Open to the public, the house is worth a visit for its beautiful rooms, furniture, and paintings.

Just before the end of the lane, cross a second cattle-grid and pass the lodge and secondary entrance to the park. The lane ends at Essex Bridge over the River Trent. This narrow packhorse bridge, which is only 4 ft/1·2 m wide, has fourteen arches with triangular refuges between each. The confluence of the Rivers Sow and Trent is just to the left, the Trent falling over the low weir.

Cross the bridge, and almost immediately turn through the gateway in the wall on the right, alongside the canal bridge. (If, however, refreshment is needed, continue along the lane to

Tower of the Winds, Shugborough
Shugborough Hall

Essex Bridge

the Clifford Arms Inn in Great Haywood village.) Walk ahead along the towpath of the Trent and Mersey Canal, with the River Trent on the right. Shortly pass under an old bridge which formerly continued over the river and into Shugborough Park. The river now draws gradually away to the right, and Shugborough is prominent on the opposite side. The high woodland seen on Cannock Chase in front is the area known as the Black Hills. After some distance, pass under bridge number 72. By leaving the towpath here and crossing the bridge, Little Haywood village is shortly reached, with its Red Lion and Lamb and Flag Inns.

Continue along the towing path. Shortly before reaching the railway bridge, note the old LNWR iron boundary post just behind the fence on the right. Pass under the bridge, and

Trent and Mersey Canal, near Colwich

shortly pass a lock and bridge number 71. The cottage on the opposite side of the lock has traditional hand-painted canal-ware for sale. Colwich church and village are also on the left across the canal. Continue beside the canal, the River Trent once again close on the right. At the next bridge, climb the bank and cross the stile on to the main A51 road.

Turn right along the road, and shortly cross Wolseley Bridge over the River Trent. Just after this, pass the Wolseley Arms Inn on the right at the junction of the A513 Stafford road. Cross over the junction, and continue along the A51 for approximately 300 yards/274 m, passing the Wolseley Tea Rooms (here venison and pheasant are on the menu) and an antique shop. Immediately after the first field on the right past the Tea Rooms, turn right along the fenced track leading to

Mill House. After some distance, remains of rock dwellings can be seen in the sandstone rock face on the left of the track. Continue along the track, which now enters a wooded area bright with rhododendrons in June. After a short distance, the track passes the old mill pond on the right. Pass through the gateway just after the woodland, and continue along the track, now with a fence on the right. Etching Hill is in front across the fields. The track shortly continues along the right-hand edge of a field. Pass through the gateway, and walk straight across the next field to the gateway at the opposite side, which can be seen once the brow has been crossed. Go through this gateway and, turning towards the left, walk diagonally across the field to the gateway on the left of the far corner. Pass through this, and walk along the right-hand edge of the following field. Go through the gateway, and crossing the road junction, take the path on the left up to the top of Etching Hill. From the rocky top by the flagpole, excellent 360-degree panoramic views are obtained. Rugeley and its power station are prominent in front, and the wooded hills of Cannock Chase stretch across-country behind. Turn sharp right at the top of the hill, and follow the well defined path which runs down to the road junction at the bottom.

Cross over the junction, and walk along West Butts Road opposite, in Etchinghill. At the end of the road, continue straight over the crossroads, and follow Stonehouse Road, running diagonally to the right. Continue along here for approximately 400 yards/366 m, and then turn left immediately after the house named Kingsholme, and just before bungalow number 63. Walk down the hedged path and cross the stile at the end of the gardens. Walk along the left-hand edge of the field, and crossing the next stile, continue along the left-hand edge of the following field. Cross the stile at the end of this field on to the road.

Turn right and walk along the road beside the woodland. After approximately a $\frac{1}{2}$-mile/800 m, turn down the first lane on the left. This is Birches Valley. After a short distance, pass the Forestry Commission Museum and Information Centre.

A few yards further, and immediately after the houses on the left, turn through the gateway on the left and walk along the good track which, bearing left, runs into the pine woodland of this part of the Chase. After some distance the track drops downhill and fords Stony Brook, running out of Fairoak Valley on the right. Cross the footbridge just to the right of the ford, and continue along the track, shortly passing a fork on the left. After about 800 yards/732 m, and just before the track ends, pass through the gateway in front.

Bear right along the road, opposite the terrace of houses. Shortly pass under a railway bridge, and continue uphill to the end of the road at a T-junction with the main A460 road. Cross this road, and turning right, walk down the old road on the left of the embankment for about 100 yards/91 m; and turn up the second of the two tracks on the left. Follow this track gently uphill along Miflins Valley, shortly with woodland to each side. At the top of the steeper part of the climb the track bears left, and is joined by another from the right. Still climbing gently, continue to the end of the track in approximately a ½-mile/800 m.

Turn right at the road, and immediately right again at the crossroads. Walk along the road for about a ¼-mile/400 m, and turn through the gateway on the left at the right-hand bend. Follow the good track down through the woodland: an electricity power line shortly runs beside it. At the bottom of the descent, cross two small streams and pass an old oak on the right. The track now climbs the other side of the valley. Some 50 yards/46 m after the sixth electricity pole from the oak tree, bear left up the initially narrow path leading into the woodland. This shortly climbs fairly steeply, and after a while passes over a cross-track to arrive alongside the Castle Ring at the top of the climb. This large ancient earthwork, consisting of banks and ditches surrounding a large central area, is the remains of a five-sided hill fort about 2,000 years old. It stands at a height of 801 ft/244 m, and is the highest point on Cannock Chase. Our path finishes at a gate leading to a car park. Walk across this to the lane, noting the excellent views over the Black Country in front. On the left of the lane directly opposite is the Park Gate Inn, Cannock Wood.

Turn left along the lane. This is named Holly Hill. Arriving at the junction with Chestall Road, pass the entrance to Beaudesert Scout and Guide Camp on the left and, continuing through the iron gate in front, walk along the fenced footpath between a covered reservoir and woodland. At the end of this path, turn right along the track. Passing through the gateway at the end of the reservoir fence, continue along the track, noting the good views across towards the left.

At the end of the track, continue straight over the road junction and walk along Darlings Lane, passing Gentleshaw primary school on the left. Immediately after the school, continue over the crossroads along the lane named Commonside, which as implied runs beside Gentleshaw Common. Pass the nineteenth-century Christ Church on the left, and bearing left with the lane, arrive alongside the stump of an old windmill, close by the Windmill Inn.

At the windmill turn on to the track running along the edge of the common, parallel with, and just to the right of, the lane. After approximately 300 yards/274 m, and opposite the junction with a lane leading off to the left, bear right along the path which runs across the common, heading down Gentleshaw Hill towards the built-up area of Boney Hay beyond the two adjacent pylons some way in front. Wide panoramic views are now seen all around from these fern- and heather-clad slopes; the spires of Lichfield Cathedral and the Trent Valley to the left, the Clent Hills beyond the Black Country in front, and the Clee Hills and Welsh borders over towards the right. Arriving at a fairly well defined cross-track running down from the right, bear left along this towards the two pylons which were your earlier marker, and then immediately bear left again and follow the less well defined path which runs down the right-hand edge of the depression on the left, heading towards the bungalow seen at the bottom of the common. At the end of the path leave the bounds of

Cannock Chase, and turning left walk along the lane beside the common.

Inn sign, Gentleshaw

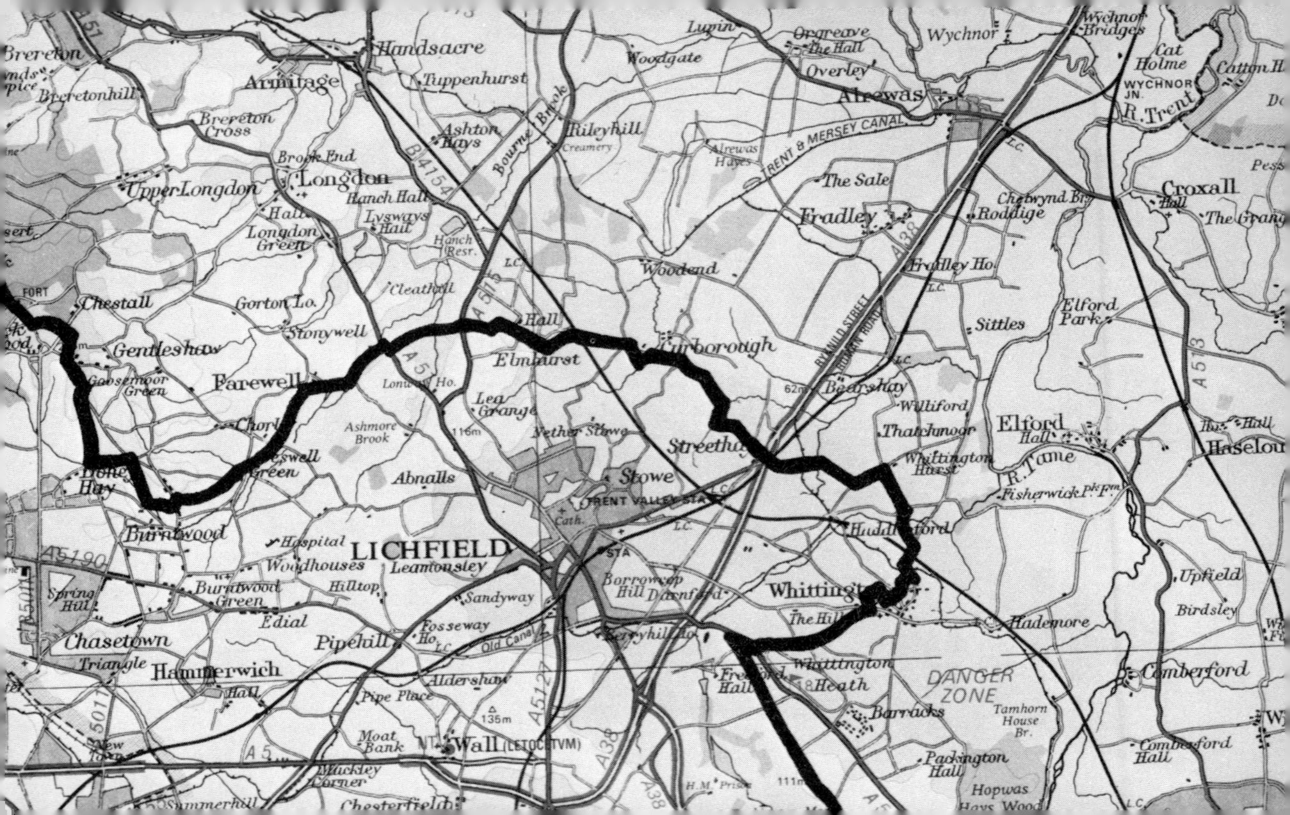

Handsacre
Armitage
Tuppenhurst
Woodgate
Lupin
Orgreave
The Hall
Overley
Alrewas
Wychnor
Wychnor Bridges
Cat Holme
WYCHNOR JN.
R. Trent
Catton Hall
Brereton
Breretonhill
Brereton Cross
Ashton Hays
Bourne Brook
Rileyhill
Creamery
Alrewas Hays
TRENT & MERSEY CANAL
Brook End
Longdon
Upper Longdon
Hanch Hall
Lysways Hall
Longdon Green
Hanch Resr.
The Sale
Fradley
Chetwynd Br.
Roddige
Croxall
The Grange
B4154
Woodend
Fradley Ho.
FORT
Chestall
Gorton Lo.
Cleathill
Stonywell
Gentleshaw
Goosemoor Green
Farewell
Chorley
Elmhurst
Curborough
RYKNILD STREET ROMAN ROAD
Elford Park
Sittles
A513
Lea Grange
Ashmore Brook
Beareshay
Williford
Thatchmoor
Elford Hall
Haselour
Nether Stowe
Streethay
Whittington Hurst
R. Tame
Fisherwick Pk. Fm.
Abnalls
Stowe
TRENT VALLEY STA.
Cath.
Burntwood
Hospital
LICHFIELD
Leamonsley
Woodhouses
Hilltop
Sandyway
STA
Whittington
Upfield
Birdsley
Spring Hill
Burntwood Green
Edial
The Hill
Hademore
Chasetown
Pipehill
Fosseway Ho.
Old Canal
Triangle
Hammerwich
Aldershaw
Freeford Hall
Whittington Heath
DANGER ZONE
Comberford
Pipe Place
135m
Barracks
Tamhorn House Br.
Moat Bank
Wall
A5127
A38
A5
A5190
Muckley Corner
Packington Hall
Comberford Hall
Hopwas Hays Wood
Chesterfield
Summerhill
H.M. Prison
L.C.

10 **Gentleshaw – Creswell Green – Farewell – Elmhurst – Streethay – Whittington**

Distance: 9½ miles/15·3 km

Follow the lane which runs below the slopes of Gentleshaw Hill, and just before reaching the crossroads, turn through the gateway on the right. Walk down the left-hand edge of the field, and continuing through the gap in the hedge walk down the left-hand edge of the next field. Cross the fence in the corner after passing under the electricity power line, and bearing slightly towards the right, walk diagonally across the end of the next field, heading for the ash tree approximately 25 yards/23 m to the left of the corner. Cross the stream and then the fence alongside the tree, and turning left walk along the left-hand edge of the following field. Go through the gateway at the end of the field, and turning left walk along Springle Styche Lane, shortly passing the Drill Inn on the left.

The lane now climbs gently uphill to its end at a junction. The Nags Head Inn is a short distance down the lane to the right. Cross straight over the junction, and follow the good hedged track opposite, known as Green Lane. Arriving at its end, bear slightly right and continue along the lane to Creswell Green and the Nelson Inn. Bear left at the junction outside the inn, and then almost immediately turn right at the next. After a few yards arrive at a third junction.

Continuing straight over the lane in front, and then immediately crossing Maple Brook, walk ahead through a short wooded area with a stream to the right. After a few yards, cross the fence in front into the corner of a field. Walk along the right-hand edge of this, with the stream just to the right, and crossing the fence, continue along the right-hand edge of the next field. Cross the fence at the end of this, and walk along the right-hand edge of the field following, with the stream still to the right. At the end of this field, cross the fence just to the right of the corner.

Crossing the lane, and the fence immediately in front, continue along the right-hand edge of the field opposite.

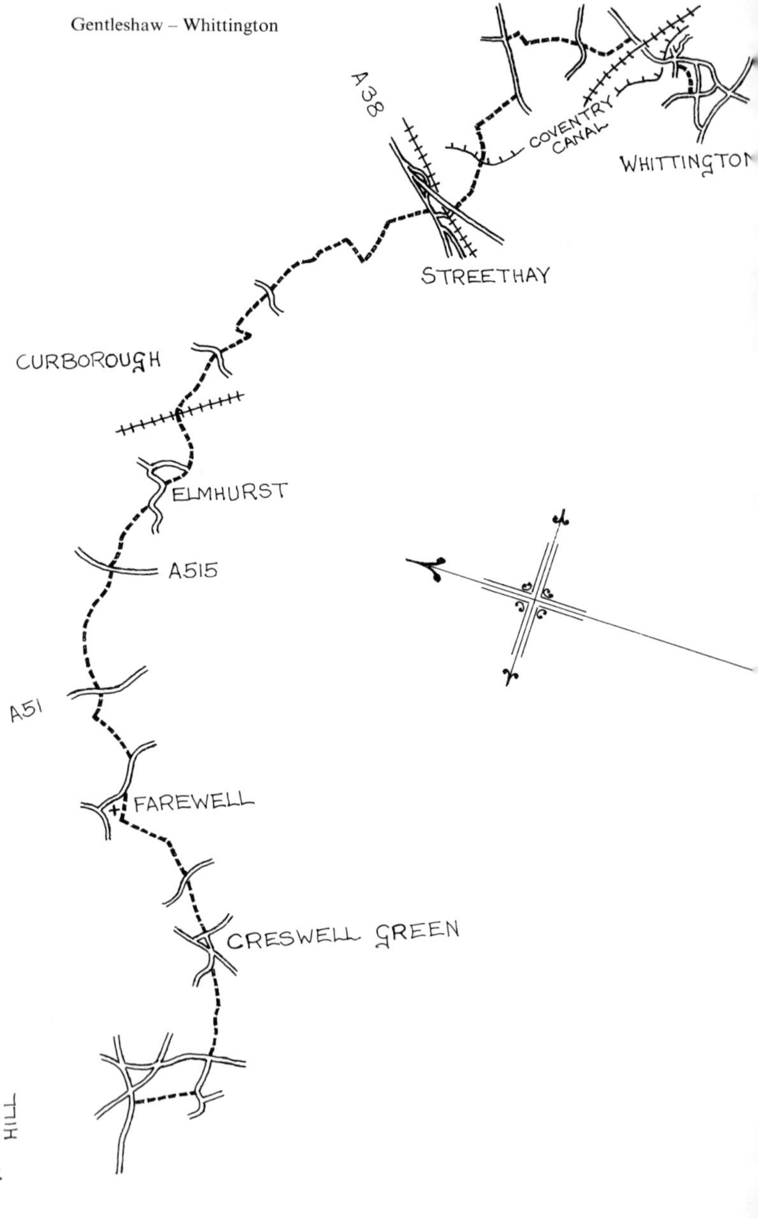
A 38
COVENTRY
CANAL
WHITTINGTON
STREETHAY
CURBOROUGH
ELMHURST
A515
A51
FAREWELL
CRESWELL GREEN
GENTLESHAW
HILL

Farewell Hall

Farewell church can be seen some distance ahead, and Chorley Place is the large house over to the left. Cross the fence at the end of the field, and heading some way to the right of the church, continue straight on across the next field, keeping parallel to the stream running along its right-hand edge. At the far end of the field, cross the stream and continue beside it along the left-hand edge of the following field. After approximately 100 yards/91 m, turn left over the fence under which the stream has just turned. Immediately cross the stream near an old sluice, into the corner of the next field. Walk diagonally across this to the opposite corner, heading directly towards Farewell Hall to the left of the church. Go through the gap in the fence here, and crossing the narrow belt of land on which trees are planted, cross the fence and continue diagonally over the next field, heading for the left-hand end of the Dutch barn at Farewell Hall. Arriving at the fence, bear right and walk along the top left-hand edge of the field, passing the Hall and farm on the left. Go through the gateway, and continue along the top edge of the next field.

St Bartholomew's church in front has a thirteenth-century chancel, while the rest dates from the eighteenth century. Farewell Hall is late seventeenth century.

Cross the small stream, and passing to the right of the church walk diagonally across the top corner of the next field, keeping parallel to the line of electricity poles which run across it. Cross the fence in front at the gap in the hedge, and turning right, walk along the lane.

After a short distance pass a cottage and an old water mill on the right, and then after about 200 yards/183 m turn through the gateway on the left, immediately before the bridge over Bilson Brook. Turn right, and walk along the right-hand edge of the field, with the brook on the right. Cross the fence at the end of the field, and follow the right-hand edge of the next, still beside the brook. Note the pool on the right, the home of numerous waterfowl. Cross the fence at the end of this field, and walking between the brook and a hedge cross a second fence, and still between the brook and hedge, shortly arrive at the driveway leading to Bilston Brook Farm on the left. Turn right and walk along this driveway, immediately crossing the bridge and passing through the gateway. Turning left, pass through a second gateway and follow the tarmac driveway across the field.

Go through the gateway, and walk straight over the main A51 Lichfield–Rugeley road, to cross the stile just to the left of the gateway opposite. Walk along the left-hand edge of the field. Approximately two-thirds of the way along this, cross the line of an old hedgerow with a few trees still remaining. Cross the fence in front, and bearing left, walk along the left-hand edge of the next field. At the end of this, cross the fence and walk straight across the field in front to the gateway opposite, which leads into the corner of the right-hand of the two fields beyond. Just before reaching this gateway, cross a small stream. Go through the gateway and walk up the left-hand edge of the field. Pass a pool in a fairly deep depression on the left at the top of the field, and then go through the gap in the hedge in front. Turning towards the right, walk diagonally across the next field to its opposite corner, heading just to the left of the house which can be seen beyond. A good view back to Cannock Chase can be seen from here. Cross the fence in the corner, on to the main A515 road.

Cross the road, and the stile opposite—slightly to the left—and following the signpost *Public Footpath–Elmhurst*, walk straight across the field to the opposite corner, passing near an intruding corner on the left approximately two-thirds of the way across. Go through the gateway, and continue along the right-hand edge of the next field. Go through the gateway at the end of this, and walk along the right-hand edge of the field following. About three-quarters of the way along this, pass between an ash tree and a pond in the bushes on the

View towards Rugeley from near Elmhurst

right. From here, continue straight across the corner of the field to the gateway leading into the left-hand of the two fields beyond. Go through this and walk along the right-hand edge of the field. Pass through the gateway at the end of this, and continue along the driveway in front. This leads from Elmhurst Hall, to the left.

At the end of the driveway, continue straight on along the lane in front. After approximately 300 yards/274 m, and where this turns sharply left, cross the stile in front at the bend, and walk along the right-hand edge of the field. Elmhurst village is to the left. Cross the stile at the end of the field, and walk along the narrow hedged footpath between the houses. At the end of this, turn right along the lane and almost immediately, where the lane ends, bear left along the good track alongside the bungalow. After a few yards, turn left off this track, and follow the left-hand edge of the field, noting Lichfield across to the right with the three spires of its cathedral prominent. Pass through the gateway, and bearing left, continue along the left-hand edge of the following field. After a few yards pass Apsley House on the left, and then walking round the end of the house, follow the track running along the left-hand edge of the field. Pass through the gateway at the end of this, crossing the remains of a cattle-grid, and walk along the left-hand edge of the next field.

Cross the stile, and heading diagonally right, walk straight across the main Trent Valley railway-line to the stile on the opposite side, seen just beyond the stanchion supporting the overhead catenary. Cross this stile, and turning towards the right, walk diagonally across the field to the intruding corner. From here continue along the edge of the field, alongside the hedge on the left, heading directly towards an electricity pylon some way ahead. Cross the fence, and continue along the left-hand edge of the next field. Arriving alongside the pylon, bear slightly to the left, and cross the remainder of the field to the gateway seen directly in front of the farm buildings.

Pass through the gateway, and crossing the lane walk along the track opposite, alongside Curborough Hall Farm on the left. Just over 50 yards/46 m past the farm buildings, turn through the gateway on the right, and immediately turning left, walk along the left-hand edge of the field. After a few yards, where the hedge (and track) turns away to the left, continue straight ahead across the field, heading towards the prominent willow tree. Arriving at the edge of the field, cross the fence and walk across the narrow neck of the next field to the fence just before the tree. Turn left here and walk alongside this fence, with Curborough Brook to its right, to the end of the field. This gradually narrows to finish in its last few yards as a track.

Go through the gateway at the end, and turning right, pass through another gateway immediately on the right. Cross the bridge over Curborough Brook, and then the fence, and turning left, walk along the left-hand edge of the field beside the stream. After a few yards, where the stream and fence turn away to the left, bear very slightly towards the left, and continue across the field to the gateway at the opposite side, heading towards the two houses which can be seen above the brow of the field beyond, and keeping parallel to the telegraph line which runs across the field. Go through the gateway, and walk up the centre of the initially narrow field (to the right of the line of telegraph posts in the rather sparse hedgerow), heading immediately to the left of the group of bushes hiding a pond near the brow of the field. Arriving alongside this pond, bear slightly towards the right, and continue diagonally across the remainder of the field to the far corner, heading to the right of the large ash tree just beyond.

Cross the small piece of fence in the hedge at the corner, and turning left walk for a few yards along the lane. Just before reaching the left-hand bend in the lane with a tarmac driveway on the right, turn right across the fence into the corner of the field. Walk ahead along the right-hand edge of this and, passing through the hedge at its end, continue along the right-hand edge of the next field. Almost immediately cross the end of an old tarmac roadway which was once part of a wartime aerodrome. Shortly, where the hedge you are following turns away to the right, continue straight ahead across the field to the far side, passing a few yards to the right of the pond in the tree-lined depression. Cross the hedge in front—this point was completely impassable at the time of writing, and a short detour to the right was necessary. Having passed the hedge, bear towards the right, and walk diagonally down the field to its bottom right-hand corner.

Arriving here, turn left and walk along the bottom of the field; and after a few yards cross the fence on the right, immediately before the ash tree, into the corner of the left-hand of the two adjacent fields. Walk ahead along the right-hand edge of this, and at the end cross the fence and small stream. Turn right, and follow the edge of the large field, alongside the stream. The lines of poplars across to the left are

Near Streethay

reminiscent of a continental landscape. After some distance, continue with the stream where it bends to the left out into the field. After a few yards, where the stream turns to the right at the field bridge, continue along the track beside the line of poplars. Stay with this where it bears slightly right after a cross-track. Nearing its end, the track continues as a tarmac driveway alongside Streethay House Farm.

Go through the gateway at the end of the track, and turn right along the main road in Streethay, immediately passing the Anchor Inn on the right. After a few yards, turn first left into Ash Tree Lane. Follow this, and shortly pass through the gates and over the level-crossing at the Lichfield–Burton railway-line. Follow the roadway which bears left and passes under the main A38 road. Immediately after the bridge, go through the wooden kissing-gate alongside the field gate on the left, and walk along the right-hand edge of the field. After approximately 150 yards/137 m, cross the stile on the right into the next field. Turning towards the left, walk across this field, heading just to the left of the second pylon counting from the farm buildings on the right. After some distance, cross the stile in a temporary fence running across the field, approximately in line with the end of the farm buildings. Continue on, now heading directly for Stoney Step Bridge over the Coventry Canal, seen just past the bottom of the field. Cross a second temporary fence, and continue to the stile at the bottom of the field. Cross this, and then a second stile alongside the gateway leading on to Stoney Step Bridge. Continuing over the bridge, walk down the hedged track. After a few yards, and at the bottom of the slope, turn through the gateway in the hedge on the left. Immediately cross a ditch, and turning right walk along the right-hand edge of the field. After a few yards cross the end of a ditch running to the left across this field and then, turning towards the left, walk diagonally across the field to the gateway at the opposite corner. Go through this, and walk along the right-hand edge of the next field. After a few yards turn through the gateway in the hedge on the right, and immediately crossing a small stream walk ahead along the hedged path. After some distance, this continues as a hedged track.

At the end of the track, turn left along the lane—the Plough Inn is a short distance to the right. After about a $\frac{1}{4}$-mile/400 m, and opposite the first lane on the left, cross the fence on the right into the corner of the field. Walk ahead along the left-hand edge of this. Go through the gateway, and turn right along the right-hand edge of the next field. Go through the gap in the hedge at the end of this, and then turning towards the left walk diagonally across the following field to the gateway at the far corner. Pass through this, and continue straight across the next field, heading immediately to the right of the bungalow and its outbuildings at the far side—this heading is to the left of the television transmitter-mast seen beyond. Cross the stile on the right of the bungalow, and walk across a small garden area to the lane. A warm welcome, and a glass of home-made wine or a cup of tea, awaits any walker who calls on Mrs Harrison at the bungalow.

Turn right along the lane, and almost immediately left over the triangular grass verge at the bend; and then, avoiding the opening into the field on the left, walk along the narrow path in front leading through the bushes. Immediately cross a small stream, and continuing through the bushes, cross the stile into the field. Walk straight across this to the plank footbridge over the stream at the opposite side—a few yards to the right of the gateway. Cross the bridge, and then the fence, into the corner of the next field. Turning slightly towards the left, walk diagonally across this, heading for the gateway about halfway along the hedge to the right. Arriving alongside this, bear left and continue along the edge of the field. Pass through the gateway alongside Bridge Farm on the right, and turning right, walk along the lane.

After a short distance pass under a railway bridge, and then shortly cross a bridge over the Coventry Canal at the entrance to Whittington village. After a few yards, turn right opposite the Swan Inn into Swan Road, and then after a further 25 yards/23 m, turn left up the concrete driveway between the houses. At the time of writing, a small new housing development was under construction at the rear of these houses; when it is completed, the route will continue between two of the new houses on to the new cul-de-sac. Turning right, walk for a few yards to the end of this and continue to the fence in front. Turn left here and, following the fence walk alongside the last house and its gardens to turn right over the new stile into the end of the field. Bearing towards the left, almost immediately cross a stile into the next field. Walk along the left-hand edge of this, alongside rear gardens to more houses. Cross the stile at the end of the field immediately alongside the house, and turning left walk for a few yards down Huddlesford Lane, to turn right at the crossroads near to the centre of Whittington.

The church of St Giles dates from the seventeenth and eighteenth centuries.

Stowe
Whittington Hurst
R. Tame
Haselour
Fisherwick Pk. Fm.
Huddlesford
Upfield
Darnford
Whittington
Birdsley
The Hill
Hademore
Wigginton Field
Freeford Hall
Whittington Heath
DANGER ZONE
Comberford
Barracks
Tamhorn House Br.
Wigginton
Packington Hall
Comberford Hall
H.M. Prison
111m
A 38
A 51
Hopwas Hays Wood
Packington Moor
Coton
Streetway Ho.
Perry
Hopwas
The Alders
Packington
Weeford
Lichfield
151m
TAM
The Bodnets
CAS
Black Brook
ROMAN ROAD
B 5404
Hints
WATLING STREET
Bonehill
Green Barn
Bourne Brook
A 446
Fazeley
Lt. Bangley
Stockfields
WILNECOTE STA.
18
Great Bangley
160m
Canwell Hall
R. Tame
Drayton Bassett
Roughley
Carroway Head
Shirrall
Dosthill
Little Sutton
A 4097
Moor Hall
Middleton
73m
Ashfurlong Hall
118
143m
Littleworth End
Cliff
Hall
Hunts Green
74m
Manor H
Whitehouse Common
Stoke End
The Linbridge
Allen End
A 446
Bodymoor
SUTTON COLDFIELD
Langley Hall
Hemlingford

11 **Whittington – Hints – Drayton Basset – Middleton – Bodymoor Heath – Kingsbury**

Distance: $14\frac{1}{4}$ miles/23 km

Starting from the crossroads at the junction of Back Lane and Huddlesford Lane in Whittington village, walk for approximately 100 yards/91 m along Back Lane. Turning right, cross the fence alongside the gateway just after the Dutch barn, and walk along the left-hand edge of the small field. Cross the stile at the corner and turn left. Walk along the left-hand edge of the next small field, and crossing the stile at the end of this, continue along the left-hand edge of the next one. Arriving alongside the farmyard wall, bear right and walk diagonally across to the gateway at the opposite corner of the field—this is just to the right of the end of another brick wall. Pass through this and turn left, and immediately left again through another gateway on to the farm roadway. Turn right and walk for a few yards to the gateway across the end of this. Go through this gateway, and bear left along the lane.

At the end of the lane—ignoring the lane to the right—bear right along the major road towards Lichfield. Walk the length of this, passing Whittington Heath and Golf Course on the left, to its end (approximately $1\frac{1}{4}$ miles/2 km) at the main A51 road. Turn right here, and walk along the main road towards Lichfield. After approximately 250 yards/229 m turn through the gateway on the left just after York Cottage and immediately before the brick wall running down the left-hand side of the road. The Horse and Jockey Inn is a short distance down to the right.

Walk along the hedged and fenced track, and at the end of this go through the gateway, and follow the right-hand edge of the field. Pass through the gateway and, crossing a tarmac roadway, continue along the good track in front alongside the line of Lombardy poplars, initially along the right-hand edge of the very large field. The ITV television transmitter-mast at Hints is prominent in front as the track climbs gently up the

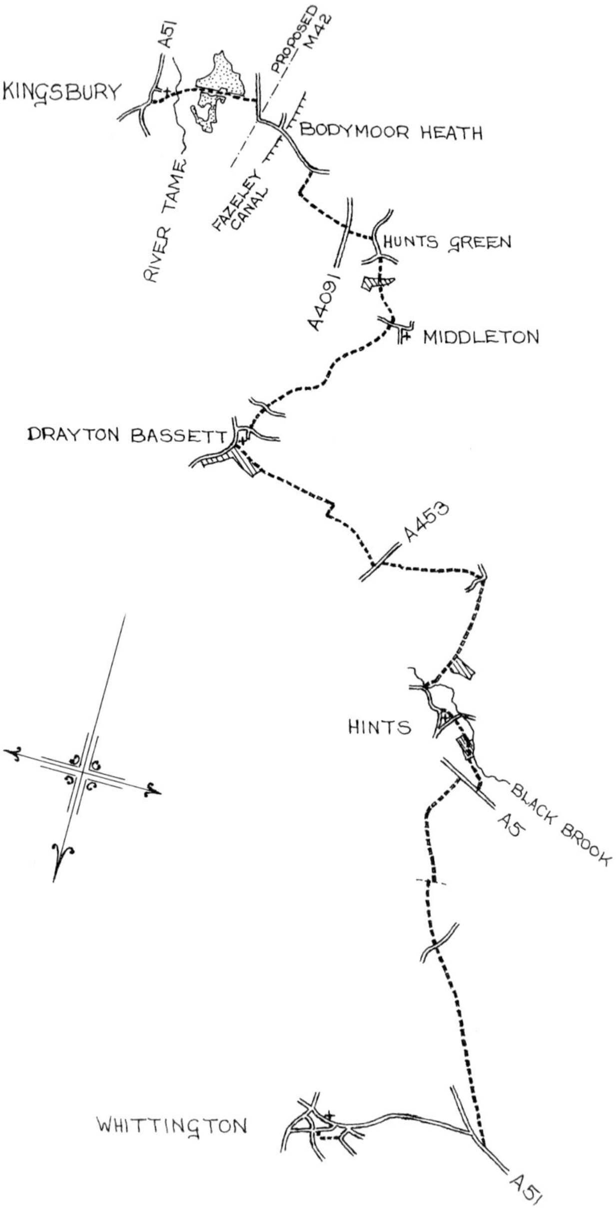

A51
PROPOSED M42
KINGSBURY
BODYMOOR HEATH
RIVER TAME
FAZELEY CANAL
HUNTS GREEN
A4091
MIDDLETON
DRAYTON BASSETT
A453
HINTS
BLACK BROOK
A5
WHITTINGTON
A51

field; and nearing the top the BBC mast at Sutton Coldfield is seen across to the right. Pass through the gateway at the top of the field, (Freeford Home Farm is to the left) and, continuing straight over the track, walk beside the farm building along the left-hand edge of the garden of the house on the right. At the end of the garden, pass through the gateway, and follow the old track along the left-hand edge of the field. A line of old elms runs along the right-hand edge of this track. The large house seen some way across to the right, is Swinfen Hall, now one of HM prisons.

Pass through the gateway at the end of the field, and crossing the driveway to Ingleyhill Farm, go through the gateway opposite and walk along the left-hand edge of the field. Go through the gateway, and continue along the left-hand edge of the next field. Go through the gateway, and walk up the old track in front. At the top of this gentle climb, cross the driveway leading to Horsley Brook Farm, and walk along the fairly short-hedged track. Whittington barracks can be seen across to the left. From the end of the hedged section, continue along the left-hand edge of the field, noting the long views towards the right to Sutton Coldfield and Walsall, and Barr Beacon with its crown of trees prominent on the skyline. At the end of the field, follow the narrow path in front running between thick bushes. Nearing its end, this continues as a hedged track finishing at Jerrys Lane.

Cross the lane, and walk along the good-hedged and fenced track opposite. After a few yards the hedge and fence finish, and the track continues between fields. Passing to the left of a small coppice, walk straight over a cross-track, and continue down between more fields. Passing through the hedge at the bottom of the field, continue with the track across the next field. Go through the gap in the hedge at the top of this, and turn right along the cross-track—known as Knox's Grave Lane—and then almost immediately turn left through the gateway. Follow the track along the right-hand edge of the field. At the end of this, continue past the house to the gateway. Go through this, and bearing slightly left, walk along the right-hand edge of the field. At the bottom of this, pass through the gateway and continue along the right-hand edge of the next. Pass to the left of the building at the end of the field and, bearing right, go through the gateway and walk along the concrete roadway to its end at the main A5 road. Maria's Cafe is approximately 450 yards/411 m up to the left.

Hereabouts the countryside becomes hilly and wooded.

Turn right down the main road for approximately 300 yards/274 m, to the bottom of the slope. Turn left here, through the gateway of the house called The Lodge. Walk down the short tarmac driveway, and then continue ahead down to the small iron gate in the fence at the bottom of the garden. Pass through this, and gradually bearing round to the left, walk along the right-hand edge of the field, following the line of the old driveway to Hints Hall, alongside an iron fence. Black Brook is to the right. At the end of the field, pass through the stone pillared gateway, and continue along the track through the woodland.

At the end of the track, pass between the two fallen pillars. and turn left up the lane. After a few yards, turn right over the stile into the woodland. Follow the path through the trees, alongside a barbed wire fence. Shortly, and having climbed steeply, pass through the gateway into Hints churchyard. Follow the footpath across the churchyard, and pass to the right of St Bartholomew's church. This was rebuilt in 1883 in the Early English style.

Go down the steps and, passing through the main churchyard gate, turn right down the lane through the lower part of Hints village. After passing through a sandstone cutting, the lane ends (approximately 200 yards/183 m) alongside Botley House. Bear right here, and cross the bridge over Black Brook, noting the old county boundary marker-post, which is nowhere near the present-day boundary. Walk to the end of the short hedged track and turn through the gateway on the right. Walk alongside the hedge on the left, following the fairly well defined track. Black Brook bounds this field on the right. After a few yards, turn left with the fence and hedge, and crossing the stile alongside the gateway in front, walk up the left-hand edge of the next field. Cross the fence at the top of this into the corner of the wood, and, turning left, cross a second fence immediately in front, leaving the wood. Turn right, and walk along the right-hand edge of the field alongside Roundhill Wood. Excellent views are seen across to the left from here. Cross the fence in front and continue along the right-hand edge of the next field. Dropping downhill, pass a pylon on the right, and after a few more yards arrive at the field corner. Cross the fence and continue straight ahead across the following field, heading for its far corner and in line with the buildings at Hints Farm some way beyond. Cross the fence a few yards to the left of the corner,

St Bartholomew's, Hints

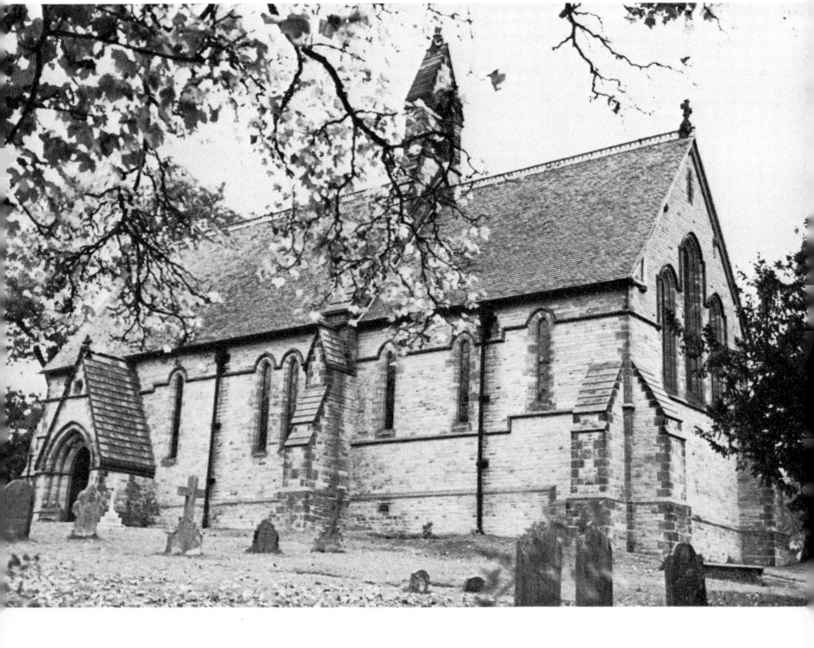

and continue across the next field, passing immediately to the left of the three oaks near its centre. Just short of the end of this field, pass to the right of the intruding field corner. Immediately turn left, and crossing the ditch go through the gateway into the next field. Turn right to regain the previous heading, and initially walking alongside the hedge and fence on the right, continue across the field, heading for the gap between the large barn (with a Dutch barn to its left) and the buildings at Hints Farm.

Arriving at the farm, walk along the concrete roadway between the buildings. Cross the tarmac roadway in front, and immediately cross the fence on the left of the bend, into the corner of the field. Walk straight up the middle of this

Roundhill Wood

field, passing a few yards to the left of the bushes just short of its brow. Once this has been crossed, continue over the remainder of the field, heading for the electricity pole in the fence in front. Cross the fence just to the left of this pole, and continue across the next field to the gateway at the opposite side. Pass through this, and walk across the following field to the short piece of fence in the hedge opposite and a few yards to the left of the oak tree. Cross this fence into the corner of the left-hand of the two following fields, and walk ahead along its right-hand edge. Go through the gateway, and continue on along the right-hand edge of the next one. Cross the fence, and walk diagonally across the next field to the far corner. Cross the fence in the corner, and continuing alongside the hedge on the left, pass the barn and go through the gateway in front, slightly to the right.

Turn left and walk for a few yards along the main A453 road. Almost immediately turn right up the tarmac roadway leading to Hill Farm. After a few yards pass through the gateway alongside a house. At the top of the hill, bear right with the roadway and pass through the gateway alongside the farm buildings. Continue along the concrete roadway (passing a pond on the right) to the gateway in front at the end of this large farm complex. Go through this, and follow the right-hand edge of the small field, with more farm buildings to the right and the farmhouse across to the left. Pass through the next gateway in front, and walk down the left-hand edge of the field. After some yards, passing a pool on the left, continue to the bottom corner, noting the long views in front with Hams Hall power station across to the right, Drayton Bassett church in front, and the tower of Tamworth church across to the left. Turn right in the corner, and walk along the bottom edge of the field, alongside the hedge on the left. After approximately 150 yards/137 m, turn through the hedge on the left, into the corner of the right-hand of the two adjacent fields—a slight detour could be advantageous, by crossing a little further along the hedge.

Walk along the left-hand edge of the field, heading for

Drayton Bassett village some way in front. Go through the gateway, and passing a pond on the left bear slightly towards the left, shortly to join the track running along the left-hand edge of the field. Follow this to the end of the field. From here, passing Heathley Farm and its buildings on the right, continue to the end of the track in front.

At the end of the track turn right along the lane through the village, passing the Post Office, and the parish church of St Peter on the right. This church has a Perpendicular west tower, while the nave dates from 1793, with a later chancel.

Continuing along the lane, shortly bear right at the junction, towards Mile Oak and Canwell. After a short distance, and a few yards past Rectory Close, turn left along the tarmac path running between houses numbered 20 and 22. Cross the stile at the end of this, and turning slightly towards the right, walk across the field to the small piece of fence at the opposite side, immediately on the right of the stone bridge.

Cross the fence on to the lane, and passing straight over this, go through the gateway opposite at the left of the bridge. Walk along the right-hand edge of the field beside the stream. This is the first of several very large fields to be met over the next few miles, which have been formed by the removal of many hedgerows between smaller fields. After approximately 200 yards/183 m, where the edge of the field bears round to the right at an oak tree, bear slightly towards the right, and walk diagonally across the field to the opposite corner; this is located between two oak trees, each a few yards on either side of the corner, and themselves just to the right of the squat tower of Middleton church, which is seen some way ahead. Arriving at this corner, go through the gateway in the right-hand hedge, and bearing slightly right, walk ahead along the left-head edge of the next field. After approximately 110 yards/100 m and just before the line of an old hedge, marked by two trees out in the field, turn though the gateway on the left; and heading slightly towards the right, walk straight across the field in front, heading for the right-hand edge of the group of oaks surrounding a pond towards the far side of the field. Pass immediately to the right of this pond, and continue straight ahead to the edge of the field, at a point a few yards to the right of a shallow corner.

Cross Gallows Brook here, and also the county boundary to re-enter Warwickshire. Walk straight ahead across the next field, heading for a point at the far side which is a short distance to the left of the tower of Middleton church. This heading brings you to a slightly intruding field corner. Pass through the hedge just to the right of this point, and continue diagonally across the corner of the next, very large field, now heading directly towards the church tower. Arriving at the right-hand edge of the field, pass through the gap in the hedge, and continue diagonally across the next field, heading for the electricity pole seen some way to the left of the church tower, approximately midway between this tower and the block of houses in Middleton village. Arriving at the intruding corner of the fence surrounding the small childrens' play area, bear slightly right and walk alongside this fence to its end at the electricity pole. Bear left here through the gap between the fences and walk along the narrow fenced path past a wooden community hall. This path ends with a broken flight of brick steps leading down to the lane in Middleton village.

Turn right on to the lane, and almost immediately turn left after the garden of Fairfield Cottage opposite. Further on along the lane are the church of St John the Baptist, and the Green Man Inn. The church has a Norman south doorway with a zigzag arch, and the tower is Perpendicular. Just outside the churchyard stands an interesting old village pump.

Following the public footpath sign, walk along the left-hand edge of the Samuel White Charity bungalows land, and, crossing the fence, continue down the left-hand edge of the field. Cross the stile and plank bridge over the ditch at the bottom of the field, and continue along the right-hand edge of the next one. Arriving at the first corner of this, bear left and continue beside Langley Brook. After just over 100 yards/ 91 m, turn right, and crossing the bridge with its two concrete stiles, walk straight up the field in front, heading for the slight gap in the belt of woodland running along its top. Cross the ditch and fence here—the remains of a stile are useless—and continue straight ahead through the woodland. Arriving at the corner of a field, follow its right-hand edge straight ahead.

Pass through the gap in the hedge, and crossing the lane continue straight along the lane opposite through the hamlet of Hunts Green. This lane is signposted *Wishaw Church*. Pass Hunts Green dairy farm on the left, and continue round the double bend. Approximately 30 yards/27 m after the second (right-hand) part of this, turn left through the gap in the hedge, and crossing the ditch walk along the right-hand edge of the field, alongside a second ditch. At the end of the field,

Langley Brook, footbridge with stiles

cross the ditch and fence, and walk straight across the next, veering slightly away from a parallel to the row of electricity poles. This brings you to a gap in the far hedge, just to the left of a telegraph pole seen on the opposite side of the main road beyond.

Go through the gap, and cross straight over the main A4091 road to the gateway opposite. Pass through this, and turning right walk for a few yards to the field corner. Turn left here, and follow the right-hand edge of this field. At the end of the field, continue alongside the hedge on the right, now walking inside a belt of young trees lining the edge of the next field. After a short distance pass through the remains of the end of an old hedge, and continue inside the belt of trees. The training ground for the Aston Villa Football Club is seen across to the right. Cross the fence in front, and the gravel-quarry roadway; and passing to the right of the hedge end, walk straight across the field in front, heading for the oak tree at the opposite side, seen just to the right of the quarry spoil-heaps. Pass to the left of this oak tree, and turn through the gateway immediately on the right, into the corner of the next field. Lower Farm is across towards the left. Walk along the right-hand edge of the field, and crossing the fence, turn left along the lane.

After some distance arrive at Bodymoor Heath, passing the Post Office on the left. Cross the bridge over the Birmingham and Fazeley Canal—immediately after this the Dog and Doublet Inn is along the lane on the right—and continue along the lane in front. At this point the projected line of the M42 motorway crosses your route, and a description of the revised route after construction is given in the next paragraph. After some distance, turn right with the lane at the works of the Midland Gravel Company. After approximately 250 yards/229 m, and immediately after the workshop and office building on the left, turn left between the posts and follow the paved footpath alongside the end of the building.

The route *after* the building of the motorway is as follows: Bear right with the lane, shortly passing the turn into the old lane on the left. Continue over the motorway bridge, and after about 95 yards/87 m turn left along the path leading alongside the end of the Midland Gravel Company workshop and office building. Follow the paved footpath.

Old and new routes now combine, and continue between fences and hedges, shortly crossing the footbridge over the conveyor-belt system leading to the gravel works. After approximately 150 yards/137 m, cross the iron footbridge over the dyke leading into a large lake on the right. The path now continues along a concrete walkway, supported a few inches above ground level; and from the end of this it runs along the edge of the lake, passing a small lake on the left. Kingsbury village is seen some way in front. At the end of the lake, cross

Footway towards Kingsbury

Kingsbury Hall

the footbridge over a second dyke, and continue along the concrete walkway, supported about 15 in/381 mm above the flood plain of the River Tame. Kingsbury Hall and church are prominent on the top of the high bank in front. Cross the brick-and-concrete bridge over the River Tame, and continue along a further stretch of concrete walkway leading to the bottom of the bank. Crossing the stream, there is now a choice of two routes up the bank. The first is to walk up the flight of brick steps leading into the left-hand edge of the churchyard, and then to follow the tarmac path leading to the exit on the left; the second is to walk up the bottom of the steep cutting immediately to the left of the steps, and passing through the gateway at the top, arrive at the same churchyard exit.

The church of St Peter and St Paul has a Norman nave; the rest, including the tower, dates from circa 1300.

The two alternative routes bring you to an open area of rough grass in front of the ruins of the medieval Kingsbury Hall. Walk ahead along the right-hand edge of this grassland, and after approximately 100 yards/91 m, continue along the track leading from the grassland past a recreation ground, to turn right down the main A51 road in Kingsbury village.

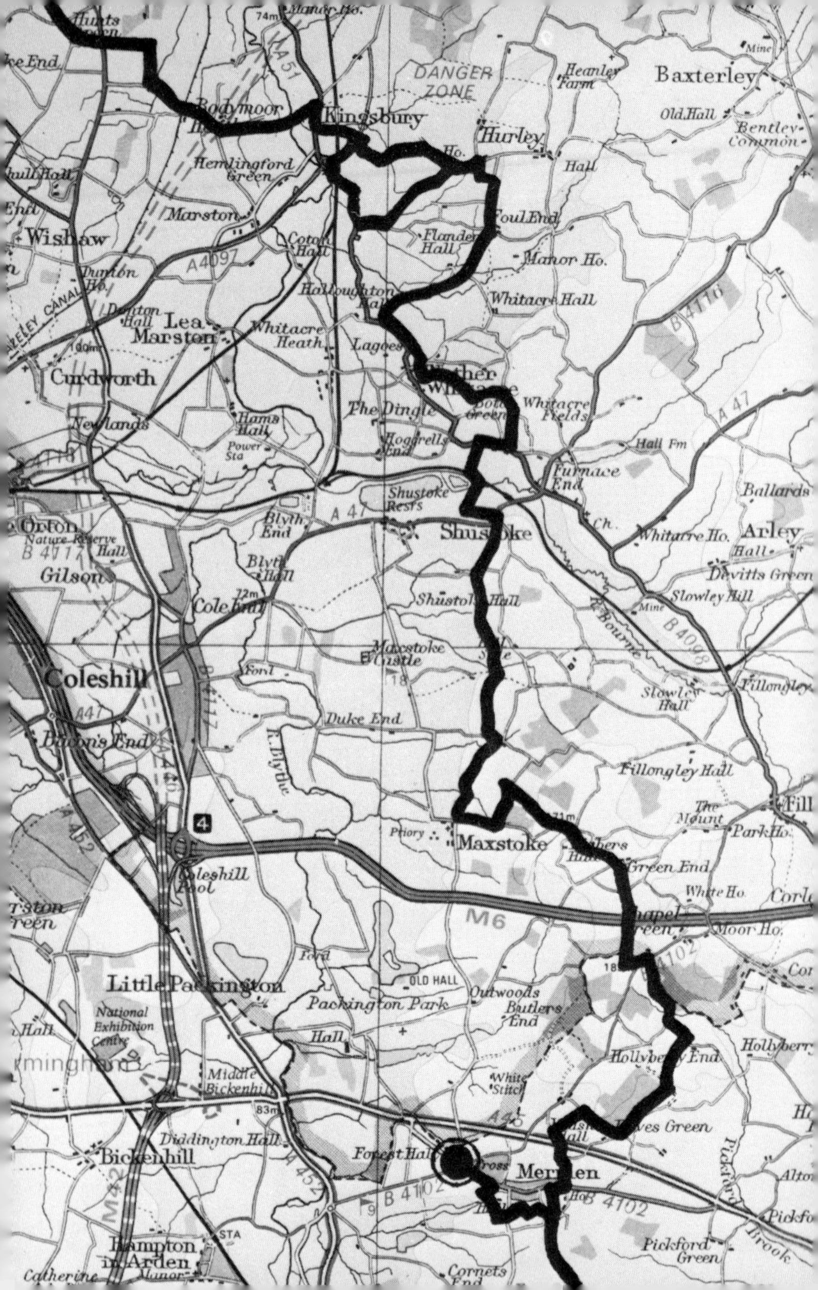
Hunts Green
Manor Ho.
74m
A 51
DANGER ZONE
Heanley Farm
Baxterley
Mine
Bodymoor Hth
Kingsbury
Old Hall
Bentley Common
Hurley
Hall
Hemlingford Green
Marston
Foul End
Wishaw
Cotton Hall
Flanders Hall
A 4097
Manor Ho.
Dunton Ho.
Hall
Whitacre Hall
Dunton Hall
Lea Marston
Whitacre Heath
Lagoes
Curdworth
Nether Whitacre
Whitacre Fields
The Dingle
Newlands
Hams Hall
Power Sta
Hoggrells End
A 47
Hall Fm
Furnace End
Shustoke Resrs
Ballards
Blyth End
A 47
Shustoke
Ch.
Whitacre Ho.
Arley
Hall
Gilson
Blyth Hall
Devitts Green
Shustoke Hall
Slowley Hill
72m
Mine
R. Bourne
B 4098
Maxstoke Castle
Coleshill
Ford
Slowley Hall
Fillongley
A 47
Duke End
Bacon's End
R. Blythe
Fillongley Hall
4
The Mount
Priory
Maxstoke
Park Ho.
Green End
Coleshill Pool
White Ho.
M6
Chapel Green
Moor Ho.
Ford
Little Packington
OLD HALL
Outwoods
Packington Park
Butlers End
National Exhibition Centre
Hall
Hollyberry End
Middle Bickenhill
White Stitch
83m
Diddington Hall
Eaves Green
Bickenhill
Forest Hall
Meriden
B 4102
B 4102
M 42
Pickford Brook
Hampton in Arden
STA
Pickford Green
Catherine
Manor
Cornets End

12 **Kingsbury – Hurley – Nether Whitacre – Botts Green – Church End – Maxstoke – Meriden**

Distance: $17\frac{3}{4}$ miles/28·6 km

Walk down the main A51 road through Kingsbury village, passing the White Swan Inn on the left and, shortly, the Royal Oak Inn on the right. A few yards after the foot of the hill, and just before the stream bridge, turn left immediately after house number 81. Follow the narrow fenced footpath between the houses. Cross the stile at the end of the rear gardens, and continue across the narrow neck of the field to the field bridge over the stream. Cross this and walk along the right-hand edge of the field, behind the rear gardens of houses. Pass through the hedge, and continue along the right-hand edge of the next, smaller field, still alongside gardens. Turn right through the hedge at the end of this field, and crossing the fence, immediately turn left and cross the stile at the foot of the embankment. Climb the flight of steps up this, and continue straight across the main Birmingham–Burton on Trent railway-line. Go down the flight of steps opposite, and crossing the stile at the bottom, walk along the left-hand edge of the field. Cross the stile immediately alongside the gateway at the end of the field, and continue over the road.

Go through the gateway opposite, and walk along the very short track leading on to Kingsbury Rifle Range. Do NOT pass through the opening in the hedge, leading on to the range; but turn right, and walk up the left-hand edge of the field, alongside this hedge which forms the range boundary. This appears to be leading towards several of the firing points, and it is rather disconcerting to see riflemen apparently firing towards you. They are in fact firing at targets some distance away and over towards the left. However, red flags are flown whenever firing is in progress, and an alternative route avoiding the range—from the point at which you crossed the road—is described after the next paragraph.

Turn left where the hedge finishes at the top of the range,

Kingsbury – Meriden

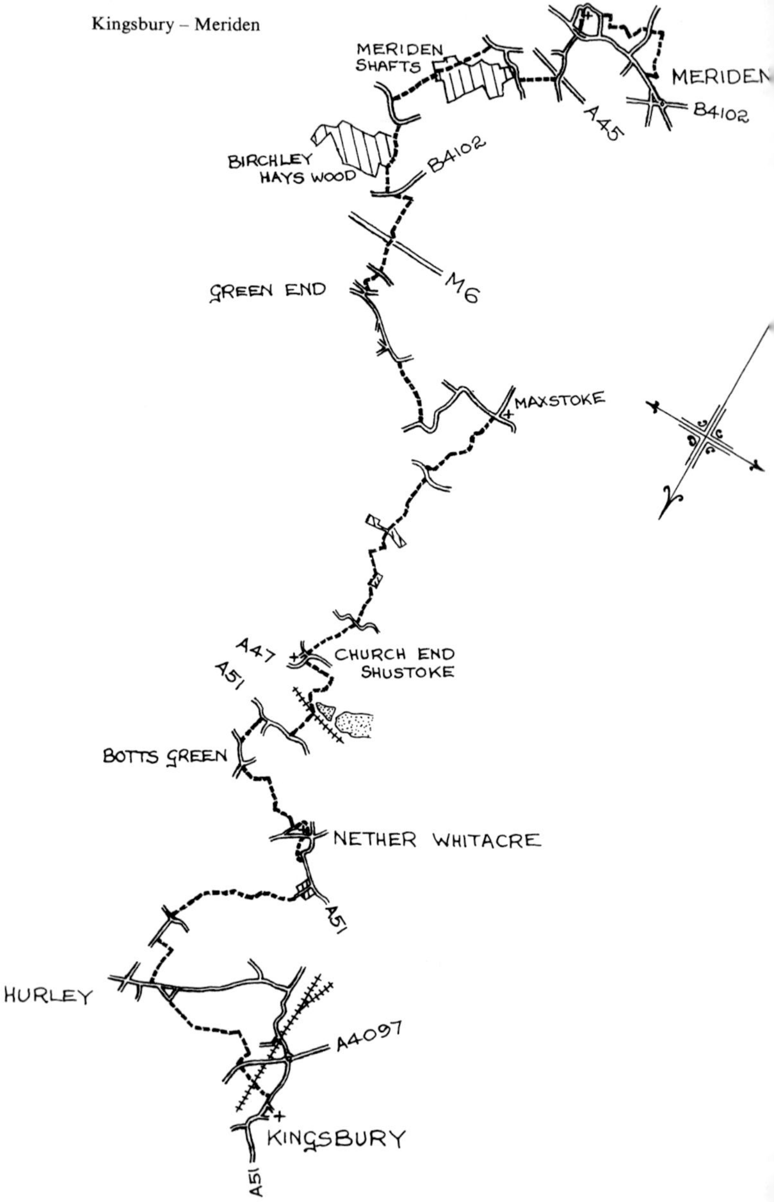

and remaining outside the boundary, continue along the edge of the field, behind the firing points. After a few yards cross the roadway leading into the range, and follow the field edge alongside a fence, noting the full view of the range seen to the left. Hams Hall power station is prominent across to the right. Turn left immediately after the flagpole at the next corner of the range, and continue outside this for a few more yards to the fence at the end of the field. Cross this, and walk ahead along the good track, running along the left-hand edge of the next, extremely large field, still just alongside the range boundary. After approximately 100 yards/91 m, and alongside the start of the belt of bushes running inside this boundary, bear right off the track, and walk across the field, heading towards the prominent oak tree which is seen a short way to the left of the buildings at Camp Farm on the brow of the field. The distance across the field to this tree is approximately 900 yards/823 m, and the actual line of the path bears round in a slight arc to the left of the direct line. Arriving at the tree, bear right, and walk beside the hedge on the left along this intruding top edge of the field, heading towards the farm a short way in front. Passing a small orchard, and a garden, arrive at the gateway alongside Camp Farm. Go through this, and walk down the lane in front.

The lane leading off to the right from the front of Camp Farm, is the finish of the alternative route avoiding the rifle range. This is now described: From the point indicated, turn right and walk along the road, which here runs along the top of an embankment, affording good views over the rifle range to the left. At the top of the gentle climb, cross the bridge over the railway, and after a short distance turn left at the roundabout on to the main A51 road, following the sign, *Coventry* and *Nether Whitacre*. Follow the main road, shortly passing under a railway bridge. Just after this, pass the end of the roadway leading to the rifle range on the left. After approximately 750 yards/686 m, turn up the first road on the left, signposted *Baxterley* and *Hurley*. Walk along this, and after about 350 yards/320 m, passing a lane junction on the right, start climbing gently uphill. After about $\frac{3}{4}$-mile/1·2 km, and a few yards before reaching the nameboard to Hurley village, bear left along the lane at the top of the climb. Follow this short lane to the point where it turns sharp right in front of Camp Farm. Here join the main route which comes from the gateway on the left, and continues down the lane to the right.

At the end of the lane bear left along the road, passing Coopers Transport Garage; and after approximately 100 yards/91 m, and immediately after the gateway on the right leading to Rockingham Fields, turn right across the fence into the corner of the field. Walk along the right-hand edge of this. Cross the fence, ditch, and a second fence, and walk along the right-hand edge of the next field. Cross the fence and continue along the right-hand edge of the one following. Good long views are seen from approximately halfway along this edge, including Hams Hall power station prominent towards the right, the West Midland conurbation visible beyond it, and further to the right Barr Beacon on the skyline. Go through the gateway, and turning left, walk along the hedged track to the gateway at its end. Pass through this, and turning right, walk along Dexter Lane.

The views to the right now become more extensive, with your two earlier friends, the television transmitter-masts, visible slightly behind you. Hurley Colliery pithead is just across to the left. At the end of Dexter Lane, now in Foul End, cross straight over the lane in front and walk along the hedged track opposite. Follow this gently down to the gateway at its end. Pass through this gateway, and turning slightly towards the right, walk straight across the very large field in front, heading directly towards the two larger chimney-stacks on the right of Hams Hall power station.

Arriving approximately at the middle of the short bottom edge of the field, turn left and walk along this edge, alongside the fence, to the corner in approximately 70 yards/64 m. Turn right here, and walk along the track. After a few yards, pass through the remains of a gateway, and continue along the track beside a stream on the left, and with a fence to the right. After about 260 yards/238 m, cross the bridge over the stream, and passing the end of a well-used track on the right, continue up the hedged track in front. Shortly, arriving alongside the houses on the right, this continues as a tarmac roadway running gently uphill through the edge of a small stretch of woodland. At the end of the roadway, turn left along the main A51 road. Hams Hall power station is here at its nearest to our route, and the spire of Coleshill church is prominent across to the right.

Walk along the main road for approximately 500 yards/ 457 m, to a point a few yards short of the sharp right-hand bend. Turn left here, and cross the small piece of fence in the hedge. Turn right immediately on entering the field, and heading directly towards the church in Nether Whitacre village, walk across the field, initially alongside the hedge on the right. Cross the fence in front, and continuing on the same heading, walk diagonally across the corner of the next field. Cross the fence on the left-hand edge of this, and continue across the following field. Pass through the small gate at the end of the narrow neck of the field, alongside the white house.

Now in Nether Whitacre village, cross straight over the lane, and walk along the hedged tarmac path opposite, leading to the church. Pass through the wooden kissing-gate into the churchyard, and continue along the path in front, to the right of the church tower. The church of St Giles is mostly of the nineteenth century, although the tower is sixteenth century. Turn left at the war memorial by the main churchyard entrance, and follow the path along the south side of the church, leaving the churchyard by the iron kissing-gate alongside the village school. Walk down the lane in front, which shortly leads to the Dog Inn; however, after about 100 yards/91 m, your route turns through the gateway on the right, immediately before the bungalow. Walk along the short grassed track, with the school playing-field on its right. Pass through the gateway, and turning left walk down the left-hand edge of the field. The spire of Shustoke church can be seen some way across to the right.

Cross the fence, a small stream, and then a second fence at the bottom of the field, and walk along the very short left-hand end of the next field. Cross the fence in front into the corner of the following field. Turning slightly towards the right, walk diagonally across this, heading towards the gateway which can be seen in the right-hand hedge just in front of a small clump of bushes and to the right of an electricity pole. Go through this gateway, and turning towards the right, walk along the right-hand edge of the next field, following the line of electricity poles. The depression immediately on the left is surrounded by the aforementioned clump of bushes. Cross the ditch and small piece of fence at the gap in the hedge, just to the left of the field corner, and turning left walk for a few yards along the left-hand edge of the next field. Where this bears away to the left, continue straight ahead to the intruding corner coming from the left, about halfway up the field. Cross the fence here into the corner of the next field, and continue on along its right-hand edge. Cross the fence, and walk straight across the narrow field to the tree at the opposite side. Cross the hedge just to the left of this, into the following field. Turn towards the right, and walk diagonally across the corner of this field, heading just to the right of the small brick building in front. Cross the fence, and passing to the right of the brick building, bear slightly towards the left and walk diagonally across the next field to the gate at the opposite corner, with a signpost prominent in the lane beyond.

Pass through the gateway on to the lane junction, and take the lane opposite, signposted *Botts Green.* After a short distance pass the half-timbered Botts Green Hall on the left, dated 1593 over the main entrance. Continue along the lane in Botts Green for approximately 150 yards/137 m, and where the lane bends left, turn through the gateway on the right immediately after the cottages. Walk along the short gravel track to the next gateway. Go through this, and walk straight across the field to the intruding corner coming down from the left. Cross the fence here into the corner of the next field, and continue ahead along its right-hand edge. Where the fence turns away to the right, continue straight on across the remainder of the field to the stile in front. This can be seen immediately at the right-hand end of the barn, itself to the left of the large white farmhouse.

Cross the stile, noting Over Whitacre church some way to the left, and going down the steps turn right along the main A51 road. After a few yards pass Botts Green Lane on the right, and continue along the main road for approximately 350 yards/320 m, to a point just after the end of its tarmac footpath and immediately before the electricity line across the road at a left-hand bend. Turn left here, and walk along the hedged track, initially past a large house on the right. The pithead gear of a colliery and Over Whitacre church can be seen to the left, and Shustoke Reservoir is through the trees to the right.

At the end of the track, pass through the kissing-gate, and crossing the main Birmingham–Nuneaton railway-line, pass through a second kissing-gate and walk along the hedged and fenced path in front. After a few yards cross the bridge over the feeder stream to Shustoke Reservoir, and bearing left walk beside this, shortly to cross a second bridge above a sluice. Continue alongside the stream, and after some distance cross another bridge. A few yards further, and now at the end of the path, pass through the gateway into the corner of the field. Turning towards the right, walk across this, diagonally to its opposite corner, passing a few yards to the right of the solitary oak tree. Cross the fence on the left of the corner and walk up the right-hand edge of the next field. Approximately 100 yards/91 m before reaching the end of this, and immediately after the pond behind the hedge on the right, turn left and walk straight across the field, heading directly towards the house seen just to the right of Shustoke church. Cross the hedge, and now veering very slightly towards the left, walk across the next field to the intruding corner coming from the right, heading immediately to the left of the church

Church End, Shustoke

tower beyond. Pass to the left of this corner, and walk alongside the hedge to the end of the field. Good long views are seen across to the left.

Cross the fence, and dropping down the bank, turn right up the main A47 road. After a few yards pass the Griffin Inn at the sharp right-hand bend, and turn left here into Shawbury Lane. The red sandstone church of St Cuthbert is a short distance along the small lane on the left. This dates almost entirely from the fourteenth century.

Having entered Shawbury Lane, turn right almost immediately over the small piece of fence alongside the public footpath sign, into the corner of the tiny field. Walk along the left-hand edge of this, and cross the fence into the next field, alongside a double electricity pole. Immediately passing to the right of the small pond, walk straight across the field to the piece of fence in the opposite hedge, a few yards to the right of the electricity pole and just to the left of a small intruding corner. Cross the fence, and continue across the next field—initially for a few yards alongside the small stretch of hedge on the right—heading for the small piece of fence which can be seen in the hedge at the far side, directly in line with a pylon some way beyond. In following this heading, pass just to the left of the electricity pole in the field. Coleshill church is once again prominent across to the right. Cross the fence into the corner of the following field and walk along its left-hand edge. After a short distance, and where the hedge veers away towards the left, continue straight on, diagonally across the corner of the field, heading for the right-hand edge of the pond in the group of trees near the far side. Pass immediately to the right of the pond, and cross the hedge in front into the next field. Turning slightly towards the right, walk straight across this field diagonally to the far corner. Cross the fence in front on to Moat House Lane.

Turn right along the lane, and almost immediately turn left across the small piece of fence alongside the public footpath sign. Turning slightly towards the left, walk diagonally across the field to the opposite corner. Cross the small piece of fence just to the right of this corner, and walk straight across the field in front, heading approximately midway between the two pylons seen beyond. Cross the fence at the opposite side of the field, just to the left of the smaller ash tree, into the corner of the left-hand of the two following fields. Bearing slightly towards the left, walk diagonally across the end of this field, heading for the intruding corner coming up from the right. Cross the fence just to the right of this corner, into the young pine wood, and continue just inside its left-hand edge.

Crossing the fence and Metlin Farm driveway at the end of the wood, arrive at the corner of a very large field. Turning slightly towards the left, walk diagonally up this, heading for the intruding corner coming down from the left, at the brow of the field. This corner is located immediately at the right-hand end of the stretch of holly bushes in the hedge. In crossing the field, pass a few yards to the right of the pond with a pylon immediately behind it. Arriving at the intruding corner, bear right, and walk along the edge of the field, alongside the hedge on the left. Following this hedge, which at first bears towards the right and then turns slightly towards the left, arrive at the large oak tree in the hedge. Turn left here through the gap, and walk out into the next field to the solitary oak tree a short distance in front. Bear towards the right here, and walk down to a point at the bottom edge of the field near a telegraph pole on the bank of the stream, and just below the left-hand end of the stretch of woodland beyond. A narrow belt of trees runs to the left from here, following the stream in its depression. Pass to the left of the telegraph pole, and crossing the stream, climb the bank, and walk ahead just inside the left-hand edge of the woodland.

Cross the fence and walk along the left-hand (top) edge of the field. Cross the fence, and continue along the top edge of the next one. The path is now climbing gently, and the views across to the right are gradually becoming more extensive. Go through the gap in the hedge, and walk along the right-hand edge of the next field. After a short distance, go through the gateway, and turning left walk for a few yards along the edge of the field following, to the foot of the bank. Turn right in the corner here, and walk along the top edge of this very large field, which, dropping gently down to the right, reveals the magnificent 180-degree view over the whole of the West Midland conurbation, stretching from the Malvern Hills away to the left, via the Lickey and Clent Hills on the skyline, to Cannock Chase on the right.

At the end of the bank, pass through the gateway in front at a slight kink in the field edge, and continue along the right-hand edge of the next field. Slightly towards the right and some distance ahead, the ruined gatehouse of Maxstoke Priory now comes into view. At the bottom of the field, just before reaching Hill Farm, turn through the gateway on the right, and turning left walk for a few yards, once again along the left-hand edge of the very large field.

Go through the gateway, and turning left, walk along the lane passing in front of Hill Farm. After approximately 170 yards/155 m, and immediately on the left-hand bend, turn right across the fence into the field. Turning towards the right, walk diagonally across this narrow field to the gateway on the bridge over the small stream. Pass through this, and bearing right walk alongside the hedge on the right for a few yards; and then continuing diagonally across the corner of the field, pass to the right of the lone tree and walk to the gateway in front alongside the holly tree. Go through this gateway, and turning left walk up the left-hand edge of the next field. After about 320 yards/293 m, and at the point where the hedge and fence turn sharply away uphill to the left, bear towards the right and walk diagonally across the remainder of the field to

Maxstoke Priory

the opposite corner—just to the right of the clump of trees at the far side. Cross the fence to the left of the corner, and walk along the right-hand edge of the following field. Cross the fence on the right of the corner into the end of the narrow neck in the next field. Turning towards the left, cross the stream, and walk along the right-hand edge of the field, heading for Maxstoke church in front. Cross the stile alongside the gate, and continue along the right-hand edge of the following field. Pass through the gateway on to the lane junction in Maxstoke village.

The tiny fourteenth-century church of St Michael, and the remains of the gatehouse to the fourteenth-century priory, are a short distance down the lane to the right.

Turn left, and climb gently uphill along Church Lane towards Fillongley. After rounding the left-hand bend at the top of the climb, bear left at the junction and walk along Bentley Lane, following the signpost to Shustoke church. After some distance the lane turns sharp right and then left. At this left-hand bend continue straight ahead up the roadway in front, passing to the right of the bungalows and to the left of Bentleys Farm. Go through the gateway, and continue along the roadway between the farm buildings. Passing a pond on the right, continue up the hedged track in front. At its end, pass through the gateway and walk straight up the field, heading for the depression on the skyline in front. The path, in climbing up to this point, runs at the bottom of a shallow cutting. Continue straight on from the head of this, heading for the intruding corner coming from the right some way ahead. A line of three oaks stand in the field to the left of this point.

A magnificent view is now unfolding behind you as you gradually climb higher up this field, with its evidence of the old ridge-and-furrow system of farming. Arriving at the intruding corner, continue up the right-hand edge of the field alongside the fence. Where the hedge and fence turn away to the right at the end of the wood, bear towards the right and climb up the steeper part of the field, once again along the bottom of a shallow cutting. From the top of this climb, go on to cross the fenced section in the hedge in front, to the right of the house beyond. Walk across the narrow strip of land with a pond on its right, and pass through the gateway on to the bend in the lane.

Bear left along the lane, and after approximately 300 yards/274 m pass two lanes on the left, and then after a further 300 yards/274 m pass a third, also on the left. This point, at 572 ft/174 m above sea-level, is the highest point that the West Midland Way reaches on the eastern side of the conurbation. Continue on along the lane for a further 450 yards/411 m, and then turn right at the next junction, signposted *Packington*. After a few yards, at the lane fork in Green End, cross the fence directly in front on the opposite side of the lane, into the corner of the field.

Walk diagonally across the field to the ash tree in the hedge at the opposite side. Cross the fence here into the next field, near a pond on the left. Turn towards the right, and walk diagonally across the field to its far corner. The line of the path is made evident by the line of what was probably an old road, firstly by a slightly raised embankment, next by a shallow depression, and then by a further stretch along a slightly raised bank passing a few yards to the left of a second pond.

Go through the gateway in the corner, and turn left along the lane. Almost immediately bear right along the track which leads in a few yards to a farm entrance. Bear right just before reaching this, and cross the small piece of fence in the hedge a few yards to its right, into the neck of a field. Turn towards the right, and walk diagonally across this to the intruding corner just to the right of the Dutch barn. Turning slightly towards the left at this point, continue across the field, heading for the oak tree at a slight intruding corner in the left-hand edge. At this tree, turn slightly towards the right, and walk diagonally across the field corner, to the gateway in front. Go through this, and walk straight across the next field, passing just to the right of the hawthorn bushes. After crossing the brow of this field, continue to the stile alongside the gateway at the bridge over the M6 motorway.

Cross the stile, and walk over the bridge. At the end of this bear left and, crossing the cattle-grid, walk alongside the fence on the right for a few yards. Cross the stile in the end of this fence—just before the start of the hedge—into the next field. Turning left, walk along the left-hand edge of this. Go through the gateway, and continue along the left-hand edge of the field following. Approximately half-way up this field, and alongside the middle of the three oaks in the hedge, bear right, and walk diagonally across the corner of the field to the gateway in the top edge. Go through this into the corner of the next field—a hedged track runs to the right at this point—and walk ahead diagonally up it, heading for the gateway at the right-hand end of the group of trees at the top. Arriving at this gateway, remain in the field, and turning left, walk alongside the hedge on the right, initially passing two ponds. About 90 yards/82 m past the ponds, and at the point where the hedge bears away to the left down the field, cross the piece of fence in front at the kink in the hedge, into the corner of the next field. Walk diagonally down this, passing immediately to the left of the barn, to the gateway at the opposite corner alongside the large oak tree.

Go through the gateway and turn left along the B4102 road. After a few yards, and immediately opposite the entrance to Hayes Hall Farm, turn through the gateway on the right. Walk straight ahead across the rather large field, heading for its far right-hand corner. This is located by walking towards the right-hand edge of Birchley Hayes Wood beyond. Approximately halfway across the field, the path continues parallel to the right-hand edge. Pass to the left of the pond in the corner, and go through the gateway. Continue along the left-hand edge of the next field, alongside the wood. After approximately 350 yards/320 m, and where the edge of the field starts bearing rapidly round to the left, bear slightly to the right and continue diagonally across the field, heading for the small oak tree at the hedge intersection between the two fields beyond the hedge in front. Cross the small and rather dilapidated piece of fence in the hedge, and then cross a small stream into the corner of the left-hand of the two fields, and walk straight up this, heading for the stile at the top.

Cross the stile on to the bend in the lane, and turning left, walk along this. After approximately 400 yards/366 m, and having passed Ivy House Farm on the left and then a barn immediately on the right, bear right through the gateway just after the end of the barn, into the corner of the right hand of the two adjacent fields, and walk along its left-hand edge. The Coventry conurbation is seen across to the left. Go through the gateway, and continue along the left-hand edge of the next field. Pass through the gateway, and continue along the left-hand edge of the one following. Cross the stile, and turn left along the hedged track alongside the wood.

After about 50 yards/46 m, and opposite the end of the first field on the left, turn right over the stile into Meriden Shafts Wood. Follow the well defined path gently down through this to the stile at the bottom. Cross this, and walk straight across the field in front to the plank bridge over the stream. Crossing this, and bearing very slightly towards the right, continue up the field to the small piece of fence seen just to the left of an electricity pole in the hedge. Cross this, and continue straight ahead up the next field to the small piece of fence in the hedge at the top, just to the left of the wooden buildings. Cross this, and walk along the left-hand edge of the following field.

Go through the gateway, and turn right along the lane. After about 160 yards/146 m, bear right at the junction into Lodge Green Lane—signposted *Fillongley.* After approximately 450 yards/411 m, and having rounded a fairly sharp left-hand bend, turn through the gateway on the left immediately before the right-hand bend and just after Walnut cottage on the right. Walk along the left-hand edge of the field, initially passing a pond on the left. Go through the gateway and continue along the left-hand edge of the next field, noting the good long views across to the left, with the tower of Meriden church prominent on the skyline. Pass to the left of a pond at the end of this field, and go through the gateway. Walk along the short hedged track to the lane, with the old half-timbered Walsh Hall directly opposite.

Turn left along Walsh Lane, and after a few yards cross the bridge over the main A45 Birmingham–Coventry road, and continue down into the valley. Bear right at the junction at the bottom of the hill, along Eaves Green Lane. Turn right at the end of this, along the Old Coventry Road. Almost immediately turn left outside the Queens Head Inn and climb the flight of steps up the bank to the New Road. Cross over the road, and go through the iron kissing-gate opposite. Walk along the short hedged path and, passing through the gate, walk up the left-hand edge of the field. Meriden church is directly in front at the top of the hill. Go through the wooden

Walsh Hall

kissing-gate, and continue up the left-hand edge of the next field. Go through the kissing-gate at the top of this, and walk along the left-hand edge of the churchyard. An excellent view is seen from here, down over Meriden village in the foreground, to the Birmingham conurbation in the distance.

Arriving at the corner of the churchyard, go through the gate on the left, and turning right walk down the lane, initially passing the old half-timbered Moat House Farm on the left. Pass the main entrance to St Laurence church, dating mainly from the fourteenth and fifteenth centuries, but with a Norman chancel. Note the old horse-mounting steps. Continue down the lane for a short distance, and then where it turns right and drops down to the village, continue straight ahead along the hedged track in front—now having rejoined the beginning of your long circular walk around the West Midlands. Cross the fence at the end of the track and, turning right, walk along the edge of the field. Bear left at the bottom corner, and continue along this edge of the field, still alongside the hedge on the right. Having crossed a temporary fence, and approximately 240 yards/219 m from the aforementioned bottom corner, turn right over the small piece of fence in the hedge into the corner of the next field—the third on the right from the bottom corner. Walk diagonally across the top of this field, to the small piece of fence in the hedge in front, approximately 40 yards/37 m down from the top left corner. Cross this, and continuing along the same diagonal walk ahead across the next field, heading some way to the right of the white cottage beyond. About halfway across this field, turn left and walk diagonally up it to the top corner in front. Cross the stile on the right of this corner, and walk along the hedged path. Turn left at the end of this (near an electricity pole), and cross the fence into the corner of the field. Walk diagonally across this field, heading for the tree which is seen to the right of the house beyond. This heading brings you to a small intruding corner. Bear right round this corner, and cross the piece of fence in the hedge in front on to the lane.

Crossing the lane, and the fence opposite, walk straight across the field, heading for the chestnut tree seen over the brow, and passing a few yards to the left of the pine tree. A magnificent 180-degree view is now seen in front. Crossing the brow of the field, a stile can be seen in the fence in front, just to the right of the chestnut. Cross this stile and, turning towards the right, walk diagonally down the field, heading towards Hams Hall power station which can be seen in the distance over Meriden village. Once the brow of the field has been crossed, it will be seen that this heading is towards the bottom edge of the field.

Nearing the bottom, pass a few yards to the left of a stone-walled corner, and then cross the ditch and stile in the fence in

Return to Meriden Cross

front. Walk straight across the next field (passing just to the right of the lone tree) to the stile in front. Cross this, and continue straight over the following field, heading towards the left-hand corner of the white industrial building in front. Immediately before this, go through the kissing-gate, and turning right walk along the fenced gravel path. At the end of this, turn left on to the end of the roadway leading from Meriden Hall. Then, in a few yards, turn left along the main road through the village, opposite the Bulls Head Inn. Walk up the road, and so return, after about a $\frac{1}{4}$-mile/400 m, to your starting point—the cross on the village green at the centre of England.

Ackleton, 121
Acton Hill, 143
Acton Moat, 143
Acton Moat Bridge, 143
Acton Trussell, 143
Adamsford Bridge, 124
Adams Hill, 82, 83, 85
Alne, River, 54, 63
Alvechurch, 67, 68–9, 71
Alveley, 101–2
Arrow, River, 67, 71
Astbury Hall, 108
Aston Villa Football Club, 183

Badger, 122
Badger Dingle, 121–2
Badger Hall, 122
Barr Beacon, 175, 192
Beacon Hill, 75
Bear Hill, 69
Beaudesert, 51, 52
Beaudesert Mount, 51
Beaudesert Scout and Guide Camp, 158
Beckbury, 123, 124
Bednall, 143, 144
Belvide Reservoir, 135
Berkswell, 27–9
Berkswell Hall, 28
Bewdley, 112
Bilberry Hill Training Centre, 75
Bilson Brook, 164
Birches Valley, 156
Birchley Hayes Wood, 202
Birdsgreen, 101, 102
Birmingham, 9, 11, 12, 23, 74, 75, 77, 205
Birmingham and Fazeley Canal, 183
Bishop Percy's House, Bridgnorth, 113
Bishops Wood, 127, 134
Bittell Reservoirs, 71, 73, 74, 75
Black Brook, 176
Black Hills, 154
Black Ladies, 134, 135
Black Mountains, 83
Blakeshall, 92
Bodymoor Heath, 183
Bonemill Bridge, 125
Boney Hay, 158
Boscobel, 11, 132, 133
Boscobel House, 132
Boteler, Ralph, 54
Botts Green, 194
Botts Green Hall, 194
Bowhills Dingle, 101
Bradley, 138, 139–40
Bridgnorth, 11, 108, 110–13, 115
Bridgnorth Castle, 110, 111, 112
Brocton, 143, 145, 147
Broome, 85, 87
Burton Green, 32
Butter Hill, 141

Cafés and Restaurants, 12, 83, 150, 155, 170, 176
Canals, 45, 46, 47, 49, 50, 73, 91, 136, 143, 152, 154, 155, 169, 170, 183
Cannock Chase, 11, 23, 75, 83, 135, 137, 139, 141, 142, 144, 145, 147–59, 165, 198
Cannock Wood, 158
Castle Ring, 157
Caunsall, 90, 91
Chadwich, 76
Chadwich Manor Estate, 76
Charles II, King, 11, 129, 132, 133
Chase Wood, 39

Chelmarsh, 107
Chelmarsh Reservoir, 106
Chelmarsh Sailing Club, 107
Chorley Place, 163
Church Eaton Brook, 139, 179
Churchill, 88, 89–90
Civil War, 35, 127, 129
Clee Hills, 75, 83, 147, 158
Cleeve Hill, 83
Clent Grove, 83
Clent Hills, 11, 23, 75, 77, 79, 80, 81, 83, 94, 99, 158, 198
Clothing, 15–16
Cofton Hackett, 74, 75
Cofton Hall, 74
Cofton Hill, 74
Coleshill, 193, 197
Colwich, 155
Coppenhall, 142, 144
Cotswolds, 75, 83
Country Code, 20
Coventry, 9, 12, 33
Coventry Canal, 169, 170
Creswell Green, 161
Crosses, 12, 23, 25, 54, 57, 206, 207
Curborough Brook, 167
Cyclists' Memorial, Meriden, 23

Davenport House, 118
De Clinton, Geoffrey, 35, 37
De Montfort family, 51
Dickens, Charles, 127
Drayton Bassett, 179, 180
Dudley, 11, 75
Dunston, 142, 143
Dunston Hall, 143

Elizabeth I, Queen, 35
Elmhurst, 165–6
Elmhurst Hall, 166
Enville Hall, 94
Equipment, 15–18
Essex Bridge, 152, 154
Etching Hill, 156
Etchinghill, 156

Fairoak Valley, 157
Farewell, 163–4
Farewell Hall, 163–4
Ferries, 12, 104–5
Fillongley, 200, 203
Finham Brook, 35, 37, 39
Follies, 82, 83, 99, 118, 151, 152
Forestry Commission Museum and Information Centre, Birches Valley, 156
Fort Pendlestone, 115
Frankley Beeches, 75, 77

Gallows Brook, 181
Gentleshaw, 158, 159
Gentleshaw Common, 158
Gentleshaw Hill, 11, 158, 161
Glacial Boulder, 149
Gorcott Hill, 63
Gortens Dingle, 104
Grand Union Canal, 45
Great Haywood, 154

Hampton Loade, 104
Hams Hall power station, 179, 191, 192, 193, 206
Harborough Hill, 87, 88
Harts Hill, 150, 152
Henley-in-Arden, 46, 51, 53, 54, 57, 63
Henry V, King, 39
Henry VIII, King, 39
Highfield, 77
Hints, 173, 176–8
Hints Hall, 176
Hob Hill, 65
Holly Hill, 158
Holy Austin rock, 93, 94, 97
Honiley, 39, 41–2, 43

Honiley Hall, 39, 42
Hubbal Grange, 129, 131
Hunts Green, 182
Hurley, 191, 192

John of Gaunt, 35
Jones, Adrian, 112

Kenilworth, 11, 30, 35–7, 39
Kenilworth Castle, 33, 34–5, 37, 39, 41
Kenilworth Great Pool, 34
Kidderminster, 94
Kingsbury, 184–6, 189
Kingsbury Hall, 185, 186
Kinver, 94, 97
Kinver Edge, 11, 75, 83, 91, 92, 93, 94, 99
Kite Green, 51

Lakehouse Dingle, 102, 103
Langley Brook, 181, 182
Lapley, 136
Lapley Manor, 136
Leicester, Robert Dudley, Earl of, 35
Lichfield, Earls of, 152
Lichfield Cathedral, 158, 166
Lickey Hills, 11, 23, 63, 65, 66, 67, 74, 77, 198
Little Haywood, 154
Loco Shed, Staffordshire County Museum, 152
Long Mynd, the, 83
Longnor, 137
Longnor Brook, 137
Lower Hall, 119–20
Lower Sherbrook Pool, 150
Lowsonford, 45, 46

Malthouse, Honiley, 42
Malvern Hills, 63, 75, 77, 83, 99, 198
Maple Brook, 161
Maps, 8, 13, 16, 17, 18
Maxstoke, 200
Maxstoke Priory, 198, 199
Meriden, 12, 23–6, 203, 204–7
Meriden Hall, 23, 207
Meriden Shafts Wood, 203
Middleton, 180, 181
Midland Gravel Company, 183, 184
Miflins Valley, 157
Milford, 143, 150
Milford Common, 150
Moat, double circular, 141
Mor Brook, 108

National Trust, 49, 76, 77, 93, 150
Neachley, 125, 126
Nether Whitacre, 193

Oat Hill, 150
Oldacre Valley, 147
Over Whitacre, 195

Palmers Hospital, 113
Panpudding Hill, 110
Penderel, Richard, 129
Penk, River, 143
Perryhouse Dingle, 100
Pleasaunce, The, 39
Pool Plantation, 137
Preston Bagot, 49, 50

Quatford, 110
Quatford Castle, 110
Quatford House, 110

Railways, 12, 13, 30, 46, 48, 57, 74, 105, 106, 108, 110, 112, 115, 125, 142, 152, 154, 157, 166, 169, 189, 195
Ram Hall, 29

Rastrick, John, 115
Redditch, 63, 65
Rednal, 75
Rednal Hill, 75
Ridge-and-furrow farming, 59, 200
Rights of way, 12, 19
Rindleford Mill, 117, 118
Rock dwellings, 156
Romsley, 76, 77
Romsley Hill, 78
Roundhill Wood, 177, 178
Route finding, 13; *see also* Maps
Rowington, 44–5
Rowney Green, 63, 65, 66–7
Royal Oak, 132, 133
Rubery, 75, 76, 77
Rugeley, 156, 165
Ryton, 124

St Mary's Abbey, 37
Satnall Hills, 151
Severn, River, 11–12, 104–5, 109, 115
Severn Valley, 108
Severn Valley Railway, 12, 105, 106, 108, 110, 112
Sheepwalks, The, 97, 98
Sherbrook Valley, 149–50
Shrewley, 45
Shrewsbury, Bishop of, 122
Shopshire Union Canal, 136
Shugborough, 154
Shugborough Hall and Park, 150, 151, 152, 153, 154
Shugborough Tunnel, 152
Shustoke, 193, 195–6, 200
Shustoke Reservoir, 195
Shut Mill, 78
Sleeper Path, 45–6
Slot Stile, 89
Smith, Francis, 118
Solihull, 11
Sow, River, 150, 152
Spring Hill, 150
Stafford, 141, 144
Stafford Castle, 141
Staffordshire and Worcestershire Canal, 91, 143
Staffordshire County Museum, 152
Standing Stones, 79, 83
Stocks, 28, 42
Stoney Step Bridge, 169
Stony Brook, 157
Stour, River, 91
Stratford-on-Avon Canal, 46, 47, 49, 50
Streethay, 168–9
Sutton Coldfield, 175
Swinfen Hall, 175

Tame, River, 186
Tamworth, 179
Tar Hill, 147
Telford, Thomas, 112
Timlet Bridge, 125, 126
Tong, 126, 127, 129
Tong Norton, 126
Tower of the Winds, 152, 153
Trent, River, 152, 154, 155
Trent and Mersey Canal, 152, 154, 155
Trent Valley, 158, 166
Trevithick, Richard, 115
Triumphal Arch, Shugborough Park, 151, 152

Ullenhall, 59–61
Upper Pool, 121

Walsall, 11, 175
Walsh Hall, 204
Walton Hill, 78, 81
Warley, 11
Warwickshire County Council, 42

Waseley Country Park, 77
Weatheroak Hill, 65
Webb Stone, 138, 139–40
Wells, 28
Wenlock Edge, 75
West Bromwich, 11
West Midlands Metropolitan County, 9, 11, 192, 198
West Midland Way, The, 9, 11, 13–14
Wheaton Aston, 135
White Ladies Priory, 129, 131
Whittington, 170–1, 173, 175
Whittington Heath, 173
Windmill Hill, 77
Windmills, 65, 125, 141, 158
Wolseley Bridge, 155
Wolverhampton, 9, 11
Womere, 149
Worcester, 83
Worcester, Battle of, 11, 129, 132
Worcester and Birmingham Canal, 73
Worfe, River, 117, 118, 120, 123, 124, 125
Worfield, 119–20
Wrekin, the, 83, 129, 144, 147
Wren, Sir Christopher, 42, 44
Wroxall, 42
Wroxall Abbey, 42, 44
Wyatt, Samuel, 152
Wyre Forest, 75